the
ARCHITEXTURES

BOOKS BY NATHANIEL TARN

Old Savage/Young City (1984)
Selection: Penguin Modern Poets, 7 (1965)
Where Babylon Ends (1969)
The Beautiful Contradictions (1969)
October (1969)
The Silence (1969)
A Nowhere for Vallejo (1971)
Section: The Artemision (1973)
Le Belle Contradizzione (tr. R. Sanesi, 1973)
The Persephones (1974)
Lyrics for the Bride of God (1975)
The House of Leaves (1976)
The Microcosm (1977)
The Ground of Our Great Admiration of Nature (w. Janet Rodney, 1977)
The Forest (w. Janet Rodney, 1978)
Birdscapes, with Seaside (1978)
Atitlan/Alashka (Alashka with Janet Rodney) (1979)
The Land Songs (1981)
Weekends in Mexico (1982)
The Desert Mothers (1984)
At the Western Gates (1985)
The Mothers of Matagalpa (1989)
Seeing America First (1989)
Home One (1990)
The Army has Announced that Body Bags... (1992)
Caja del Rio (1993)
Flying the Body (1993)
A Multitude of One (editor: by Natasha Tarn, 1994)
Poems 1985-1998
Three Letters from the City (the St. Petersburg Poems)
Selected Poems

Translations:
The Heights of Macchu Picchu (Neruda) (1966)
Con Cuba (1969)
Stelae (Segalen) (1969)
Selected Poems (Neruda) (1970)
The Rabinal Achi, Act 4 (1973)
The Penguin Neruda (1975)

Prose:
Views from the Weaving Mountain: Selected Essays in Poetics & Anthropology (1991)
Scandals in the House of Birds: Shamans & Priests on Lake Atitlan (1998)

the
ARCHITEXTURES

Nathaniel Tarn

1988 — 1994

new west classics 1

chax press   tucson   2000

This book is the first of the New West Classics series, from Chax Press. The book has been printed in the USA by Cushing-Malloy, Inc.

Supported by the Arizona Commission on the Arts with funding from the State of Arizona and the National Endowment for the Arts; also supported with funding from the Tucson/Pima Arts Council.

Poems in *The Architextures* have previously appeared singly or in groups in:

Archive Newsletter (UCSD, La Jolla); *Conjunctions; First Offence* (Canterbury, UK); *Hambone; Mandorla* (Mexico City); *Notus; OArs; Oblek; Po&sie* (Paris); *Shearsman* (Plymouth, UK); *Ribot; River City; Scripsi* (Melbourne, Australia); *Stiletto; Talisman; Temblor; To; Tyuoni; American Contemporary Poetry* (in Russian), tr. by Vadim Mesyats and Tatyana Beylin (Ekaterinenburg) 1996. *Architextures 1-7* has appeared as a deluxe letterpress edition by the Ninja Press, Sherman Oaks, California, 1999.

Chax Press / 101 W. Sixth St., no. 6 / Tucson, Arizona 85701-1000 / USA

ISBN 0 925904 28 7

Library of Congress Cataloging-in-Publication Data

Tarn, Nathaniel

    The architextures : 1988-1994 / Nathaniel Tarn
      p.cm. -- (New West classics ; 1)
    ISBN 0-925904-28-7
    I. Title. II. Series.

  PS3570.A635 A89 2000
  811'.54--dc21

               00-022652

For Janet Rodney

ONE

THE MAN OF MUSIC

ARC 1 - 7

Isn't it the end now, isn't it the way you come home as if you were not coming, as if you were staying down and were going to eat of that food for all time, what is it, the amaranth seeds, or poppy seeds, or the marigold seeds, something intolerably like that, and would be satisfied to stay down there forever, without anything to say to yourself in this new tongue, this novel we are trying to talk up here, or to say for yourself, to tell us in unwearying detail, what it is that our time needs to know that is so close now to finishing without ever having had its say?

Isn't it the truth now: that we no longer surmise where we are? That the art no longer knows where it is, that the art is repeated over and over, that the city has to be abandoned to its aging, a brand new city going up beside it, to explode into this century which is so late in manifesting? Manifesting its particular commitment of the environment to the setting and the setting to the environment, so that we have at last, what is it, a story told, a narrative in building?

So that you ask yourself, looking out of all the windows of the dead, one after another coming to each window, parting the curtains, shrouds over the windows' eyes, looking out onto that void, trying to make out the contours of the new city — but with the angle always wrong, the new buildings being just out of eyesight, just out of the field of perception — you ask yourself: what is that being, that very pale being, are we that being, that ghost almost, what is that being trying to come up very slowly into the upper air, and is she making it? Have we determined it is a she, is she making it, or an it, or a he, or, is, she, making it, or we? Is she reaching that upper air, is she coming up here to say something to us, is it true that at last she is coming home, is she coming home, is she home, is this her here beside us? Looking now back down in the opposite direction, proud of her raising herself to this unlooked for stature, of having made something out of herself, and out of *you* into the scenario?

How is it that this man of music reaches all the world, by coming up out of his own earth and going into all the various territories, taking that music with him? For it is not like language which stops you, like a door you cannot go through — but like a transparent curtain, a veil, you go through with the greatest ease. And here is the heart of mankind beating from one end of a great city to the other which is the whole earth now, where all roads spider over the planet, roads so wide you can see them from any other planet, however far away, and how marvelous it is that all this could be done with music.

It is also true that the music had to come out of the graveyard: opening the iron gates of the graveyard, every one of the stones within cleaned, polished, the names memorialized, flowers arrayed under every name, under innumerable winter snows: so you issue from that place and the understanding that the place gives you flows without impediment into the music. So that everywhere you go, they bring you tributes of flowers, books, pictures and everything that summons up the holy name of music and everything in the round-about universe that nurtures music: memories, thin and thick sadnesses, knowledge, disaster, eschatology — and it is all full to explosion with a love of life which almost sweeps you out of existence and into... into *what*? Into what else is there but this existence? What else is there but the distant sound of justice?

And she, does she remember stones moving when the music played, animals leaning on their paws, attentive to those strains? Remember the people there, quietly beginning to dance and does she see those birds in the trees swaying, those fish in the river meandering by, sinuate this way and that to the music? Look up at the far star fields sensing them, can it be possible, move into time to the music and, moving thus, generate their own music, and does she, seeing all this, finally know whether home is on this earth and is she joyous thereat? Go up to the lead dancers and bow to them, and then, secure in and of her own place, begin to lead the dance in a quiet kind of triumph as if any time in which she might not have led it had been forgotten, so much forgotten that they will say of it: look, this was nothing but a dream? Something which, pulling it apart, you'd call a vanishment?

Where is the edge of the new and where do we go in this immensity which tells us we move from one place to another, instead of moving inside one place which is always recognized? How do we know that we go from the known to the unknown, and has this new place not always been inside us since the beginning, that we go from the safe to the unsafe, the adventurous, the chivalrous, the quest, and are not draped in the safe, hide-bound, cloth of gold, tailored its thousand pieces like to a robe of abdication? When is it that we are in our landscape, full of rural preoccupations, and that we then move toward the urban threshold, manifesting a city's future wholesomeness in the traffic patterns of our brains? Is this *città nuova* or *città antica* and who can guarantee it either way? Out of the mouths of angels at every gate, flaying passers-by as they are chased into this agglom-eration, what is it that chorals assent and willing servitude, glows out in a breath of fire toward those latter distances, the maps of everything we have deserted forever?

How did we stand still and how then did the whirling universes stop flashing past us small as the daughters of our eyes? To grow, outward into that dense immensity like to an ocean crystallized, a frozen summation of geography, giant vision of every planet in the galaxy, galaxy in the cosmos: how did our stillness breed this colossus — and why do we ever bother to read another single word (or to write one) where there is enough here to last in the diction of it for inexhaustible lifetimes?

Where was she: still or running? Frozen statue of a running girl, frozen in bronze and in ice covering the bronze — that day in the park which taught us childhood, chilled even more as the girl that was perpetually running away from us, flying away from her frozenness in space and in time: we that were supposed to be the ultimate freezing agent, the megalomanic oppressors and paralyzers of everything sentient? When, already, inside there, turning around that very moment at the apex of flight, there was a body, hers, flowing out of the metal, curving, to begin the run back toward us, to return to this terrestrial island, to come back once again and forever to this home, at the center of everything, whose image all along the paradox of her flight she had never been able to flee from, had never shaken from her, never let go of, nurtured like the vision of a paradise to become?

Who is it came out of deep night gloom from the far south to beat the embattled north back into the pole, lies waiting on his bed through the long day, all blinds drawn, waiting, shutters closed, for night to come again? Goes through in his head all the medecines he had studied before his combat days, swallows drugs with a fierce will to turn his piss from blood back into gold once more? Punched around the kidneys, thrashed to the floor in his own waters pooling, exits alone, ramrod-backed after defeat, through the dark entrance hall, dark corridor, into dark night, boarding the bus alone to move back south where his name has just been deleted, memory obliterated, where his head has been sacrificed after the lost game, where his page has turned white?

And how did we stop in the middle of our own defeat, looking at the old man preparing our coffee behind the counter? The coffee of the younger man sitting beside us who did not want to be with us because we foretold his own defeat, heaping insults on his soft underbelly, but had kept company with us out of a sense of brotherhood defeated? How had we come to ask about the man who had grown old in war and who now, sensing our interest, had started smiling in our direction with the smile of an oriental sage? How had we spun to look at the tablefuls of men gambling behind us, how had all of life suddenly desisted on the blank screen and philosophy suddenly made her entrance into our totally barren existence? How had the survivor's star shone in our dead eyes, our staggering bravery suddenly flared across the sky like summer lightning?

How did she come down then, in the likeness of a sodden, burnt out, cooked, bleary-eyed, howling and whining vampire, to tell us that we could rely on her indefinitely, to the very end of the struggle and how did we tell her, our hearts going soft as we turned to add a quarter to the music, that she could rely on us without conditions to the very end of history? How did we swagger into the night which had become an interminable day, only for us to be out there some time down the road, her dark southern lover back with her, throwing our storage in our faces with some delicacy, some apology, as we came to claim rags and belongings only a few lives later?

And who, then, are these people who have been to the land where we once went, and above all, these children who have spoken to those we once spoke to and who now all look as if they are our children, adding this sense and that clarification, this context here, that underlaid assumption there, and who are begging to make our house look like a home, not a shack made of a piece of wood each from a multitude of forests (one piece each, which is all that we had time for, being then the sole explorers of that planet)? But it is also true that the house is being taken from us and is going to bear other names than ours, unless we were to enter those forests again, like the lion awakened, and make them ours: Oh! but we know the temptations of those forests — forests of study in which a thousand years are but a day, where nothing is ever written down but the throat's chord alone is all of law forever, so little one advances in any kind of knowledge that has not to do with the core of the wood — and they have no time for the trunks or barks, or branches, let alone leaves or sweet sap of the heart's scholarship.

But was it there we had wanted to go in the first place? Had we moved north, at that beginning, it would have been because we had planned, *ab initio,* to go south; if south, then north; if not west; if not east... How is it that we had never gone where we had longed to go? That we had never had our fill of desire in that matter? But had only been where others had wanted us to be, told us, ordered us to be? Done the dull deeds they had damned us to? And then, one night, after a lifetime of security, even that place, the one we had made our way to, was taken from us. Like bodhisattvas, exceedingly intelligent, skillful in means, sterling in compassion, to tempt one away from ownership, subtracting this from such and such, and that from this other, robbing everything from everyone in a monstrous round of plunder, they had come to take this place from us and give it to those who could only love it, understand it, know it less — but perhaps require it more?

And she, was she there? In what shape was she there? Was she there in the image of the carved dancing girl on the walls of that colossal temple, the one the peoples believed had originally been let down from heaven? To serve as a model of earth? Little did they know she had come up from the underworld and that her toes, very low down in the carving and hidden by the irresponsible jungle lianas, had actually burgeoned out of roots and branches from the forest floor! Ah, but is she here now, more secure perhaps because of those earthbound roots! From here there is no exit at the last, press whatever key you may into the document, and you remain firm there for time so long it must be tagged immeasurable. For to be free of it, so great a boon, that is not thinkable in this determination: no code will outreach to support it. You move through the placental text of her dispensation, not through invulnerable air.

Where is the place then of such knowledge, and what its quality, that seems to unroll like a ceremonial carpet, each one of whose designs knows the other, or like a loving river, each one of whose waves knows the other, so that no matter how many designs there are, or waves, the whole, when known, is of one piece and of one peace also? And how is it that this exists apart from us, though depending on us, continuous to roll through the years, though there may be many gaps, many interruptions, much forgetfulness on our parts, so that we, at times, literally do not know or recognize the thread of the discourse of it: yet, there it is again: that unity, cohesion, relevance of each part to each, making these waters unlike any other, as if you could tell the differences of water! Out of what mothering wisdom does this river flow, greeting what father king in his absence, birthing what princely child, father and mother both to us all?

And why do we walk out from this water, forgetfully, fitfully, why is it at times that the water means nothing to us, as if we had never been in any way baptized, authored or explicated — as they say of the ribbon of text: explicated — why is it that it has at times nothing whatsoever to do with us, because we move in a simple fashion, with the voices of children around our heads like wreaths, ah, if it were but music! and with an utterness of being in the — where is it? not mind, heart, navel, no but such entire presence of roundaboutness, of encompassment, salve on skin and air skin moves through — where all is loss gaining upon loss:

And she, is she not the first loss; is she not the loss turns aside the moment anything is born, the last fairy no one has invited to the feast, who gives the meanest gift, the dumbest present: and would you have had her give the passage, or perhaps the passion? Does she not take you down to the dead before you have even taken the trouble to be born; is she not standing there pointing the way east, sure sign of return to him who has moved west all his life, who lives below the last wall of the sun, that sun hiding its dreadful eyes so that the ending of this plot remains unknown? Is it not the case that she complicates matters unceasingly by her interminable simplifications: last, perishing enclosure, that seed alone might live, in the single ply bright air we drink of momently or die?

ARC 7 : 88

Who are we that fled the thousand lives we did not lead in order to escape the very one life that we were destined for? Who after years, centuries, aeons of fleeing, suddenly, in one moment, in a garden, a public park perhaps, felt cornered by that one true life, reeking at us from everything surrounding: trees, bushes, lawns, benches, people sitting there, children playing with hoops, skittles, or little yachts on the pond, windows of houses overlooking the park, potted nightingale-flowers tucked into balconies, servants living under the roof and looking down onto the park, wishing they could take the air out there — and we were overcome by a smile so vast we had not enough mouth to smile it, with all our teeth shining like white suns, the way they shine in the new countries, on the new beaches, *where the new nations rush along the strand in their joy*? Who went to those countries at the time of their "liberation" and asked of them whether men still feared death now that they were part of everlasting life — to come home saddened, reporting they still feared death and that the human condition had not changed?

Who wrote innumerable words adding up to something we felt a part of, in whose reality we sank with coolness, gratitude and the immense comfort of those who have at last found home, whereas all the countries surrounding us withered into a perpetual frost and the houses we had lived in became encased in ice, the memories of those who had known us mirrored over like ponds in winter — geese only shattering the silence, turned south over our frozen decoys?

How did she then, belonging to the people for whom mind is an insult and not the ultimate glory of our state; how did she come down, supposedly to comfort us, with her hoops, bangles and rings, prodding us interminably into jumping, into leaping through these rings that she thought were fire, which would test us and prove us and make us into man — but only lifted us aloft from the true conflagration, flew us above our burning sense of the one life lived, turning liver to salt, spleen to white flour, seeming to challenge the lilies of the field, white on the white expanses, their whys and wherefores, their lovely concentration into falls — of cowardice, of petrified desire?

TWO

Italian Sequence Comma with Italian Words Stop One Stop

A RC 8 - 14

Stress on seven intense from plethora of clocks. Had he been there another hour would they have stressed time too? For now, weight lifts from a familiar recital: organization withers to rest. Maternally for him it can do nothing more. Weight sinks back then — and flowers of glory waver on the abyss instead. His radical surprise! Force of decisiveness! It is as if they were names: in his mind, will it not be so with their perfumes? Letters of these names hard to abscond with, yet he has known of their alphabets always. It is only that you have to follow the aleph with the beth — and so forth down the years. He found it very needful to seize this hour before such buildings claimed him. You arrived in that somnambulant pink air Pleasance was famous for — although it was at least seven of evening and you knew you had been granted into another world.

Grace of that new root which is so old in him, it is his anchorage: he always cuts from it! Here he is, so clearly assisting his own birth. Maternities pour down afresh from all his ceilings; showered with infants of all sexes as if in a squall of flowers. Is it not the truth these people mastered size as no others have? Seize the hour! For buildings here are larger than any made in his own era. He may run the danger of disappearing into them forever, dissected in small corners no one would ever recover. Buildings smiling down on small, cross towns around them, huddled from roof to roof, swarming with dwarf contentions: have you noted how they speak to each other in streets and *piazzas*, these folk, as if there were time for nothing other than to be violently born? Whereas his people! As if manifest destiny existed in silence — unspoken, unspeakable, the very alpha of wealth itself! As if they had not precluded wealth by concern for no other repression!

Is it not frequently that "to write" is an act which is not to be followed by "to read", unless a "to read" were to be experienced as a "to write"? But this would alleviate from the original "to write" would it not? If such there ever was, would it not? But they do not know that there was such an original ever. Thus do they not retreat over and over? Until they reach no beginning — and, in that circumstance, come to understand there is no other life?

Where to enter the round? Round? Comfort to think "round" but may be line instead, interminable, and, at that point, will it matter where you enter or leave? Would it not have been wonderful to feel secure with no residue whatsoever? He had tried sunlight, a father's road. Had held father as if holding sun, but a dead sun, in his night realm not his day, bundled, mummified. Poured out love by night impossible by day. Refused to respond. Come out then *en trompe l'oeil,* holding his hunting lance, girt with horns and hounds, and could be seen far down a closed-off access, in one of the private rooms, making toward the round. *A la Veronese.* Gods peeling off the ecstasy, falling on them like rain.

Huge sunflower fed by force. Over and over had he not let himself be born as sunlight, stealing through windows, pooling over white ceilings until he had them chastely changed to gold? Understanding this play of space in time. Space speaks to space as actors on stage, treading an adequate distance. Whereby enduring vistas held, that do not shift or break, rising straight always, no matter from what angle. Now you go into endless colonnades (a colonnade interminate itself, leading into another likewise, the product of these likewise). Orange and red throughout the city, sun melted into walls, each one standing in for a dream. Your passport is your innocence and grace. This city. Other cities, above, below. All visible avenues (and the invisible) leading away from this scenario. Had you not, on a map, chosen the semblance of a circuit, closed, irrefutable, and seen but fractions of the possible? Whenas all roads now led into a parliament of gold. Thinking "*Gloire, gloria,* glory." Ceilings burning, your neck aching as you look up at them. Immeasurably they drink up your eyes. Singing etches a life into a likeness.

Whereas if the finite become smaller and smaller until you look into the very intervals of the world's body, is it not so that this vastness, this golden universe, will shrink into a minuscule stone, incandescent with wrath? He ushers in the other accredited worlds. Side by side, crushed into images, these stones shine forth together. From domes, like novel galaxies. Brighter than desert nights falling apart with stars.

E quel mistero: how had they ever fallen to this life? From high domes, those you do not examine, in forgetfulness, so close you are to walls, to center stage. Emperor throned on eagle wings; sun weighs on horses, hanged man, head broken on the balustrade, falls to distract your own. Blinding white wall brings out the mandorla of empire: plangent honors, legions at exercise, caracoling horses, shimmering uniforms, somber wine tunics, red or blue, awash with gush of silver. Cannon, sabres, lances, pikes. Always the eagle's shadow to bewitch the plains. Out of the mountains, armies waterfall, cavalry cataracts, artillery blares with the long roar of thunder trapped in crag coffins. Dancing along huge fronts, a godlike forehead moves to the smiling plains of our most memorable country. Did he not always seed imperious republics: shining, fresh-minted coins of his new currency? Pigeon-bosoms heaved. Arts praised.

Intimate fountains. Wine pours from sexes, breasts and mouths to escalating moss. As once the milky way expressed a goddess motherhood. Stairs rise and fall from fountains up to doors now leading nowhere, through halls grey with dead voices, ghosts packed into old cradles. Leaning against the balustrade over these hanging gardens, stares down into the lake ringed with ancient counties. Seizes from castle, keep, tower, villa, palace, names needed for a story told in so few days. Were you not able then, two hundred years later, to follow his round, digest his plot, intimately desire each of his characters? Who had launched himself from the glorious wings of his new empire when it had first begun to dawn over interminable sleep?

What he liked about these gardens. That they came down to the water as lip meets lip, no intervening cut or noise of street along the kiss. Small blue pavilion against the lake knits sky to water as the swallow will, housing a choice of ancestors. And the light struck her, overdone in her laces (the real had rushed to all extremes), but light had struck her from behind her shoulder, against expectancy, with such a tenderness, marble had come alive. So much a mother might have kneeled one night over an infant's bed, time leaning into sightless eyes, perfume alone afire as if with light. And he had done with conquest then, though conquest not with him — shaken he was by it until he died.

He stands in ravishment of this country. Sleep given back to him by the epiphany of it: never need he fall again — as long as he can somersault from vision to vision. Imperia to rule his vocables wherever on the map. So early, stretched its wings over the land, this aegis. So early covered all the goddesses, bound them to bridle. Scaled thighs, standards inclined between them, advanced at siren moats. Whole palace painted with these *amorini*, flesh ridden divinely. Ransom: states soon break down, family-choked so many centuries, when other eagles swoop to reunite them. After which, a great farce: empire in fascicles. Now, the whole nation perpetually restored. One third of monuments green-gauzed, gnomes busily unseen below. To see or not to see: the cosmic lottery. Country falling to pieces, in repair, invisible (all the time); fleeing him (most of the time); refusing him (some of the time). Anxiety force-fed between fish-scale thighs, for the almost unbearable weight of worship carried there.

Nth legion about to leave *PI/PR* or *PA; RA/RI; VI/VR* or *VE*. N captured troops, *la fanteria* tails between legs, stubs up their assholes — who had been writing pre-verbal testaments. Courtesies wear the stars one by one in their velvet earlobes. Catastrophic rain: the town falls over in its sleep. Unable to assimilate more monuments that day, over to acquisition. *Cartoline? Si — di aviazione — per favore.* Shops had reached out to them, window by window, purchased them in — both in the general and the particular. Whose currency privates despised on this occasion.

He in front, forehead of the tale, light-hearted, ever newly-born, young, flourishing, *cammina di pari con la Natura.* Ah, morning freshness! Dawn poems written only! Renew those days (so long ago) when eagle-claw could grip his shoulder — anywhere... the most unlikely places... pitch him bodily in. Kingdom of the holy word, moving from sight to sight! *Sine qua non* his sight. Feet, as if argus-eyed, bearing him on. Burn down insulting darkness! Torch temples where enthusiasm has absolutely died! Let in the light, more light! *Francisco! Domenico!* Here would Imperia arouse herself again: labor light lights in air, on earth, in heaven. Lineage depend from it.

To banish annoyance. So near the workplace, these pleasure-palaces, to singe a city with joy. As if roses were brought here after hours, hour after hour, wherever you were to be, no sooner opening a little than taken off, replaced. Deep blood of rose, like blood to him, arterial progress! Schematize the months. Ingratiate the gods at sky-level; your governance in symbols at the belt; choice moments of the royal life down here on earth. Munificence. Justice. Righteousness. Administration. After which, a joyful massacre of birds and animals. Some darker sport: running of idiots on mules, whores and heretics on foot, chased down by stallioned courtiers. Races in the so-called "humiliating genre", *le gare umilianti*. Upsky, of course, paradise: soul meets with soul, discourse is through the iris, love would rather pass through the eye of a needle than risk a loss of heaven. Your lords and ladies progress, drawn by unicorn, swan, eagle, lion, dragon, ape. Through their heavenly bodies, as water falls, to the plots below: are they as informed as this, ever, as fortunate?

Spring lips he could not reach though he longed to. Subsistence economy of thought alone. Informing the gentle face he saw each day, in and out of sight: he would have had her swan-drawn if he could, all the hours of her life. Facing her on his knees, full-armored and yet chained. Who came with roses crowned, on dove-winged air, breath warm with breeze, perfume on woven waters. Where he stood before his own subservient form, hands raised in blessing. Who had been brought from hell live and triumphant: by whom you think, by whom the air repeated: should you not smile on me whose epigraph is music?

Self-concern to the winds! Move out of body's burden, leaden breast heavy with worldliness; step in front of it, naked to the hilt. Armor kneels behind you, empty as air. Mandate all thoughts back to that weight, servants to scullery. Mind owns that leaden one; let him look to and after it, above and under it: you are in no case sullied. Light shines from back of *you* now, shadows *your* shoulders as you bow to her. Summer lips reached as arm crooks over neck, no matter face desired pensive to one side; her hand as if embarrassed that will soon caress, gesture learned in a school for ladies largely since. This kiss outlasts a culture as they witness it. They learn it on their lips.

ARC 13 : 88

Siren noise outside, robin clatter nearby, sleep into waking and back to sleep which would go music music. Tapestry of one texture as if woven in water. As wood falls from mountain crest above green lawns, so thrush song to lake in a rush of quick trills. From bird to bird his canto goes as two will mate with veers of white wings. No architect resists this edifying air, ghost thread of mortar through imagination: the only buildings which cannot fall, or be pulled down, or added to by others. Through which song echoes — as if all operas were being played together in a dream, none warring with another. Such space for music, depth in the terrasphere, no singer flies alone but, in marvelous choirs, spreads satin voice over all your stairways.

Whereas, in cities, the infinitesimal souls of dogs look up at him from cobblestone or pavement, weaving along beside their masters, full of their own preoccupations, caring no jot for palaces in air he'd raised day after day on *terra ferma*. Who remember waters in which they'd swum, canals through which their paths had been appointed when all these millenary houses had dumped their surpluses to flush land dry. But, perhaps, you will have thought, these are very large, capacious souls — huge souls compared to yours. Conserving plans of immemorial cities: avenues, crossways, streets, parks, plazas, pleasure groves, numberless cuts through lots linking one to another. See, once for all, how dog eyes meet at their own level, deep layers of conciliation in them from centuries of care, and tell if you do not believe eyes meeting high above them are not more full of murder and assassination.

Had he not promptly decided, on realizing the grandeur of this task, that, were he to miss one, two, or three of these cities, it would not greatly matter? Since they'd be launching other voyages and would invariably catch themselves up? While on this very expedition, had he not planned these subsequent, for fear that, once returned to their own home, they would have lost the necessary details? Did he not own vast repertoires of cards, slides, indices, guides, catalogues and maps from which to draw *periploi* for failing memory? Too, there were matters of advancing age which threatened to curtail all explorations. So, likewise, he took counsel with authority, contracting that if he weren't to see some cities in this life, he would reincarnate in the vicinity to see them in the next — and so forth till the repertoire of cities should be entirely exhausted.

How they rise, one after the other, like clocks at small intervals, these voices sounding deed as sole measure of day! How they lay ambition to sleep in modest achievements! Raised this great helm of the extended world that nothing can depart from, circumscribed glance from single possibility: the planet has looked you in the eye and blinked: enough! you have changed time to gold and purchased vision from... a holly leaf! Free (inasmuch as conscious of volitions and desires) men had thought themselves. But, ignorant of causes by which led to desire, they do not even dream of their existence. Now stand these palaces erect against your woman world as generals advancing to their lands with casual caresses. Avenues part, lined with tall trees, let buildings in, vistas of generation open beyond the property. Pillars march martially into the city's thighs and you can rest now, declare day vanquished, *passeggiare.*

Whereas striving for wisdom is the second paradise of the world. Master of staring eyes sees not in this domain; questions won't stretch as far as this, nor any research whatsoever. Gloriously have you departed into the silence of pure sound! Capitals crumble that were built on desire; the city is sold to broker and pawn; shares in her tumble to deserted streets; rivers surrounding her float cat and rat to their graves; ocean awaits it all with open arms — until the sea itself dies of these fabrications. And there *he* is, our Zeta, asleep in his tree, held in his forest! Her boughs encompass him, lyre music only he can soar to, hear on the midnight wave. How moon struck through her boughs that night of nights, winkled your heroes out singing for renaissance, while an exhausted mist covered the lake and no shore shimmered from the further side!

Sometimes, you will see need for courage nowhere described in any human book, pleading the divine. There will be those to have made bread, in time of famine, with no tangible flour; wine will have flowed, dark as the west where ocean had been clarified with sunken bells. You will have looked again over the landscape and with astonishment noted it had not changed one jot. His voice known as sole agent of any transformation. *Lascialo! Lascialo* (be!) None will have come to feast beheld as he had been beheld — whose step drew out no mark in sand, breath moved no air, touch raised no welt on fire, mind moved like water surrendering to water.

THREE

ITALIAN SEQUENCE COMMA WITH ITALIAN WORDS
STOP TWO STOP

ARC 15 - 21

One sky is rich in each of them, undivided: together men fashion one heaven. Let him focus on eye who would divine this human. Look deep into one gaze, face-to-face world, who would see first effect of inspiriting fire. Dwells on this, reports it fully: in every detail, every circumstance. Explores alternatives: how gaze said also this (a little hidden); that (quicker to manifest); the other (perhaps in rhyme, or even quite contrary): a master has no fear of contradiction. Little by little adds accretions until you have a picture from one gaze akin to single sky, reflecting altogether. Fame springs full-armored from this gaze as girl from father's thought, spreads on "our hills, our valleys" a full geography. Houses, villas, palaces; canoes, clippers, ocean liners; cars, trains, zeps, airplanes, gather together names culled from these pages: chapters, book of the book your culture reads from. Happy who names partita, sings for the planet!

Where there floated, still on still water, some fishing boat with the name of a father sung through those parts for omnivorous kindness. Where, further on, sprung out of bay or inlet, entered the fast yacht *Innominato* carrying manifests of a spectacular conversion. Where fishing nets had names like heroine, hero; king, queen; prince, princess; pope, cardinal — liberal lists of those who hang men from their power like flies suspended from the sun. Or bait from flashing lines over motionless silver. Broad scimitar, sundering mind cleaving created from uncreated, while the rest stay mired in primeval sand.

Thus the huge world is closed so nothing can leave it: one single number should determine their life. Greater than one has no rest, death coming on from inside him, not from the savagery he faces daily in that gathering darkness. And they, still bogged in shades of explanation! Had he not begged to be granted a few acceptable poems that he might not be ashamed in the eyes of his fellows? And they will speak to him of "inspiration", "cause and effect", the "scintillating triggers", attempting to pry loose how mind will run like rivers, fishers of music and mens' thoughts. More and more joins he less and less; will not flatter his way into your charitable graces; question a vision he wants in no way answered; attempt to pry the pearl from any dungeon. Sings trap, cage, prison bars, by preference. Light grows in darkness, heart by heart won over, time steady in its means, mercy becoming. If he sees home only once more, he cannot perish.

Here a thing is in wholeness of being. By looking you will tell all can be known of it. At worst, all there would be to know were history replete: if you had stomached centuries, years, months, days, hours, minutes, whole. If fractions of the whole had cast their faces at it, now castling back at you. Harvest plentiful, storehouses abundant, grace of your sovereign lord adequate to this splendor: he has given out, you have received. Immemorial problem of that which is that (I am that I am) in no wise otherwise. Land in which beauty can be comforted by (almost) endless knowledge. Had he not known for certain that self would no way serve to ground a culture on, would pay no interest beyond, save endless repetition? First: inveterate restriction of universal doings to the scissors of self. Second: bespoken jacket, cut to set you straight, puts him, west by east-west, into a plotter's prison. Next, vocals of old *ding an sich,* tuned to a new world's chords, performed thrice or *quartetto* by these filial fathers. Lastly: self auctioned off, naked, to rooting *hermeneusis.*

People outside derivative, lost in possessive's *piazza.* And obdurately blind: "This likes us not my lord, we comprehend it not. We do not read it. Do not receive it. We do not read you, over." As when you cannot see from your house to his house, your lawn to his lawn, shopping basket to shopping basket. Best-seller instead. Last night's video. What you can say to each other because you saw it together — though at similar times in different houses. Not in *stesso corso, stesso stradone, stesso viale,* eye to eye, mouth to mouth, ear to ear, reduction of distance. Cable no street, *pace* all mediation.

Felt this and that. Thought was it this or that. Understood *tutto bene. Niente, niente. Dolce far* you know what. Nine hundred pager at the end of it (some at this very desk): can you envisage a nine hundred tusker with trunk still beating in the midst of them? When even maestros had not gone beyond a ninth to a tenth? Trunk looks for understanding it can feed its mouth with among such self-defenses. *Mamma mia!* Alarums and excursions *Mallarmamia!* And exeunt severally. Where was air then, beaten to all enchanting canon by the vulgar tongue? Where was the vulgate tree, its voluptuous branches, its leaves at the end put forth unsullied, as if... on overdraft? You shall not see it again, short of a revolution.

Train within train, motionless motion. If he goes to such places, where goes he (where gone, where will go) goes no place? Arrow of aimlessness from no eye aiming — but blind eye to bull's eye outvoicing him back. So, fifty years after, a modular park: travel and end there, child broken to adult, his faces in facets, father to man? Past, lodged behind sight, advancing to present, into his dross, encounters memory: and what had it been exactly memory held, fixed *mezzo-secolo*, memory begged for? Things cut to his height, hugely high to that height, isomorph to that height, looking up at his eyes? Far remembered aright, near remembered awry: what hole had mind dropped in — to childerness resting? Crumbled, dead buildings, pulling down present. Train outside train, motionless motions, signal lights draining this night of bright darkness.

How was he moving to water, by way of arrival, stressing the water moving to lips of land? Where plant fell to lawn, lawn lapping at water? Sweet land, where pain of beauty could find some joy in pain — as long as it were pain of limitless knowledge! As plant had been land's water, so fish now water's land — but how to find fish where water's all fish, has taken on entirely the becoming of fish — to the latter exhaustion of aquarian wholeness? Then is the danger of no eyes passing, cut of discretion between sighting and sighting. *Et in pace requiescat.*

Who had arrested informational progress, stopped for a moment oncoming even time — dangerous train (*pericoloso sporgersi*), debris of early language threatening from? Had he not said "I love trains. That go, stop, arrive at particular places"? Who tongued no speech born, no crystallization, no water to harden in breach of quick action, quick life of a muzzle lifted through ice? How to stop that progression? Dive again, deepness a threat to dissolving, plunge plow below wave to stop profound ocean, churn depth at a core where spider trips furrows, water-web weaving from sprouter to planting. Water won't harden, nor freeze at this juncture: water stays motionless, motionless moving.

Had he not ventured: "only with music do it so that all might hear — and damn the brazen specialized ear!" Meantime, unknown to anyone, paths had collapsed. Villa to lakeside tower, then boat to lap's edge, delivered them into lake, eaten out the sun's eye (all this being anything but mind and mind only). From ore make lore, store at your peril. Whereupon, sleep had raised him to the power of dream. He had asserted old rights while naming no names: number of mother, son, dutiful ghost — to which you can add implied, furtive, father. He admitted that because of i) waxing Kabbalah and ii) increasing isolation from any genuine world, he had given himself up to exclusionary exegesis and the production of professorial fodder. As for the south: they had paved their canals; plague had ensued; rebellion exploded; invaders been tortured; flags despicably torched. Now their armies swept irresistibly north to slam against the Alps, invading history to do it evil turns and put all poets to slumber and snore.

Tenderly then, had she not bent from her mooring, sun pouring down in streams over her shoulders? Clothed with that shawl of waters, had she not wept on him — that had never adored her? While a furtive father, wrapped in mustachios, hunched in his toga, out of fashion for him, looked out the other way toward the *forestieri*? Should he have attempted to bring the world to heel within a single sentence? Even as the coda lathered his flowing hair, he had grown resentful in his vespertine grove.

Oh! Oh! you do not believe he could have said that! Philosophy he would have had to use but not believed in it! Credences would have had to have elapsed! Conjunctions; temporary cytoplasmic union; sulphurous fusions of similar gametes among inferior phallothytes; temporary cytoplasmic temblors with exchanges of nuclear material — all would have had to be arrested! It is not credible that any catacombs should have subsisted. Not under pressure exerted by the south! Alexandria passing. Come lovely evening, open thy thighs to him who would be born of vaginocracy — and let it not be said they'd not defended things when they had only meant to fertilize ideas!

Addio, mountains thrust from water into sky! Fierce peaks known to your *cognoscenti* alone, impressed on mind as clear as lover's face! Torrents he tells as well as fast familiar voices; hamlets scattered like flocks over the silver hills! The more he moves into a plane, the more his eye lours at its uniformity: air lifeless over glooming cities — house subtracted from house; street worried out of street; *piazza* withheld and bracketed from *piazza* — wounding thin breath in callow lungs. Gawks at the monuments *forestieri* admire, wondering why; recalls more restless now God's little acre. Cottage he could recycle if only he might find the gelt at rainbow's end. How wealth loses charm at that fell time; how much he wonders why he ever wandered; how willingly he'd turn again back to the granite wall — but for that hope of homing filthy rich!

Had there ever been a way out from city to jungle? Could he have crossed the possible white town (he had hit on a Sunday and gone right through, without ever meeting a living soul) to take that nightly plain bound for the tropics? In spite of having warnings of coups d'etat? Of revolutions? Round trips from countless borders under armed guard? Tanks in the streets; hackjobs through jungles with machetes; false scents deposed to faze the dogs; secret meetings called on forest edges (there where the land plunged down from mountain air)? And seeing, far, far down the glistening distance, hillock on hillock roll to the grand river, before the final wall, his own house stand to heart of no place known, no map dictating it, no longitude to pin it down to latitude's ease...

Glory be! You had made it back: without swimsuit; blowgun; parachute! Nothing uprooted. Not one fish disturbed. No animal roused from its lair; no bird rushed from its treetop — not even a mosquito set abuzz from cattle skin or wattle. Had he not walked right through imagination without one dent in the environment? Had it not come to this: that everything could be surmised bar toil and trouble; that everyone could sleep now in the house without concern; that poems could be read on the following day as if they were the most important fruit of mind — mind set in its acceptance of dynastic truth? What he had always secretly fought for? As if no one at all, but absolutely no one, had been abandoned in those forests, high on those mountain tops, looking down into several neighboring nations, biding *your* time?

Not these times again. Grey city. Never these times again. Grey city. Never this glory more: Carlo, Luca, Piero, Andrea, Giovanni. Never this genius again. Never these secret services. Not this blue again, not this red, not these greens. Generation of fruit out of stone, flower from metal, musical goldfinch, nightingale; eloquent mouths singing silently his golden legend. Stone elegance, man minted in jewels. Tenderness falls through milk night; hand held to breast pointing it out. Child grasping breast, looking at you, demonstrates you. From which stars expressed. Flip coin to flagellators motionless dancing, knight drawing sword to swat grey prophet. City divine modestly centered, motionless, meditates. Egg over shell in space and child, thrown on her knees like a lap rug, asleep. Profoundness of that sleep discovered where all point, while angels watch you watching them.

As if they had been looking at him not from this, but from another, life — and were talking him, not unto this life, but unto another. Knight donor turned aside in meditation, full armored, gauntlet to ground, not looking — attendant. Nose hooks sex in the rug, draws it toward him. This talks too. Not this blue again, not this sky; not this red again, not this blood: not this grey, dove-breasted, between indifference. Outside, against grey city, afternoon rust. *Lepri:* seven thousand five hundred a kilo. *Fagiani:* sixteen hundred a kilo. *Quagli puliti* : one thousand a piece. *Passeri* : two fifty a piece. *Tordi spiumati:* thirty five hundred a piece. *Germani spiumati:* fifteen thousand a kilo. *E la faraona*? Domesticated! Fall from sky drenched in blood over a turntable, shot into city shops, eyes autumnal. Tears rise from lake to overcome city.

Because life with himself had always been the worst he could think of, has traveled, explored, moved around overmuch. And had he not known it kept genius alive — (more than bran, incest and company) — he would have put an end to himself a long while ago, perchance by some kind or another of suicide. From prophecy: a name, or place, or poem, he'd just been thinking of. Ahead, a bookstore greater than any. Universal bookstore in small locality. Locating books ten years before their need. Forestalling the inexpressible boredom of heaven. Not these times again, never such times again: not this trinity more. No expectations. No terminus in sight.

Autumnal leaf smell all round. Thin warbler note ten degrees thinner than her previous star. Shall he sign this wall? Not on his life if he wants to return! Does he want return? Doubtful — but time won't introduce itself: you never know whose agent waits to do you first and foremost. No, not sign the wall — or, if sign, then small sun in the top right corner. As on another lake: *et ego* there. Let that be said for the imagination! Haze over lake today; visibility nil; total shut down of flight: mind only here surveying tree-tops through which invisible cultures are about to shine. *Ah lascialo clamar' quel' infinito* because of tragedy incised into his fate! You shall go now. Go down now. Back into desert. Back to the wall where sun is always dying, at least in memory, set to a forward clock. No! leaving no remembrance best: the noisiest alive are the quietest dead — and, if that is not the case, *e ben trovato*. Bring out the wine and drown the mastersingers. The orchestra stands or falls by osteonecrosis. Geriatric idiopathic osteonecrosis!

Had been a game once. Nominate your house — deepest and most profound of houses — and most un-named. Let there be one large house (gigantic hallways, myriad rooms, millenary stairs, infinitude of corners recondite with marvels). Each corner of that house packed with collections: books, *objets d'art*, tapestries, pictures, ephemera of every kind — loot of *all* nations, *all* catalogued and cared for by expert regiments slithering round their designated orbits. He owns it all — and them. Continuity, consistency, collegiality, with hosts of dedicate computers surveying most worlds. Leading down from this mansion goes a small path, gliding until mansion becomes invisible. Small lakeside, small hut, totally empty. Which is where he survives by intimate preference, at all times wavering or beating back the dark.

How well it would have been to come back one day, anointed with triumphs, one more time again! Rehearsing empire! Had he not said: how marvelous it might be to run as a "great poet" for extended vacations at the butt-end of life? Even though the existence might not be worth the candle! But empire is dream: work for republic. So go they now (down to the lake in ships) moving to desert tongue, where sand shall drink them. Gulls flutter-fish in droves: the water's rich. Under the water, always golden sand: by law of the great personal pronoun pluralized! Dearest of homelands! No longer darkness can be imagined. Go now: return to you and he, this paradise recovered. That's not the last way left to such a thing as fame?

FOUR

AMICUS CURIAE

ARC 22 - 28

Do but not be. Not be here but do there. Bring in a being, if you must, to be your doing there. Be-lieve here. You're not believed there. Here does not speak you or speak with you. Leave here and dwell there. Where for whatever reason you are not believed, nor even listened, nor lastly heard to, while chances of retrieval retreat for afterglows no one will credit. But there you are (here you go) — core of some inconceivable preoccupation: first atom — tone, and now atone — first star, first minute of (say) first four minutes, at this decisive, unquenchable throw! And none to witness it. So sit in power seat, so speech there. Or voice of music: that knife without a hilt. Grey here, green there, winter and summer under single wrap. To shore where heart endeavors thoroughly, move there, swim there, fly that green shore. Ground green on grey: come into possible through parted curtains, come into possible out of paradise. You will recall it was exile there already: they show you from exile into exile. Do paradise will do, not be it — that is dream here, that is not do there, or ultimately doing.

An Herzland vielleicht. Look out for time there: you know this is not time. Here "time" stands like a stone alone. Hinge of stone. Even stone in air is solitary, continues stone, however high, unheard by air around it. Where even dust assumed his light of once upon. But if that stone can deter light, and not fall back, well, on that stone can you not paradise again? What is that "do" if not his gift of time? Made whole, as it was once before emergence? They move to you here as dreams do primary, not talk, not address, not recognize of you but — passing, always passing, through nightly mist, black mist of understanding. Lie under you, crushed, weeds coming again. Oh! there you are! Ha! Freewalk, freewheel, and he did not see, expect, invite you to pass by here, to inhabit his dream. Not even were he hand could handshake flower here: he will not see a single winter hand advance to his in dream.

That face there. Interminable length of animal, beast raw from evolution, lengthy in shank and tail. Tall story. Trailing no glory-vapors out of creaturehood, countless back feet mired in slime still, yet look! That face there, already come beyond! This one encounter. Backlash is flesh but face is not: a sign of paradise to do there, where time can reach again. Shall do with those of cities, however stone is hard, where men be found and moveable to do. But will, beware that. Enough for now already.

Word. Clatter word. Weigh word. Position it. Then, here take word to lips and worship it, word clothed in lineaments of clean desire: so only word is wanted, lusted for. Not to look hard at word even that close but closed your eyes to word, lips laid a little on it, hot body tucked to it, so: penetrate. Hug word, fancy word close. Have you loved less than word without your own: you worm in love? So much for *dinglichkeit.* Ah, now word bears her offspring, *une ribambelle* they used to say, and so is sentenced to a length of hardship. You gaze now on this child, now over that, sensing resemblances, snorting the wind of kinship — until sense groups itself around you and you serve, as jury both and judge. And what you knew *before* you figured word, or while you met it, or even afterward, how does *that* clothe when winter want blows cold? Nothing prevents you from a turn of page: but, look, they troup again, closer this time, informed by page before, threatened by page to come. Many a page to come weighs on your knees: scarcely a winter blanket to your desperation?

And he enquired: why did you never name them? Whom you committed to a fouler death than all technology could bring them to? That question! By failing this one word: to unremember it? And he waited. For all his length of life, to be so moved! Oh such precise awaiting! For that annunciation would bring a color back to his lay universe! He sees request in his eyes that turn almost to hers, who had always awaited, whose fate was to await whatever might come by. Which, without here, will never touch her — but sail on by as if it were a dream: never to impregnate. To have missed a friend, sailing the night of a whole life, not meeting with those eyes, which thus requested. And he waited on.

For if he says to you: but be it pain, or be it sufferdom, whatever by this face is promised to a word, or by a word, into time's belly — come now, remember! Whisper with wind these names till wind becomes his name, turns rings round planet of blind acceptance. But he humored him not: air stayed stagnant. Voice pleaded with silence without prevail. So quietly he stepped into the water which bore him off within the names he premised.

Weather no wise has an account with him. War begun among heavens (great thunder at outlying seasons), third world, third war that is. Today he gave his life away for a song but paid a man who took it. Analysis requires construction of 1] Structure of field of philosophical production; 2] Structure of academic field; 3] Structure of field of power. From this to that and back to this again, whole structure of collapsing time-machine. On no account mess with this man unless you are knowledgeable as he. Which clock broke our philosopher on his own wheel, speech coming pure, high toned — in the form spider, in the form swastika.

Beware materialists without materials: this is no work for you. Beyond you must go, over two breasts ever in opposition, to which no third breast — no hospitable middle — can be attuned. Down through valley of death ride to seat of creation. Ride on right wings of revolution: find positive and negative in bed together. Turn your hard back on culture. Sink into inner revelation transcending all systems: follow arduous gurus and esoteric maestros, bugger four neo-shamans, suck off sweet animal, wrap a medecine tree, worship a whale, sacrifice his hunter. Back in nature the pure, the undiluted! Man is not born and has not been for several million years. What you have here is beast, violence prone.

Hyena hides in woodpile, drinks lives as they fall through the hollows of his hide. Beast as sterile as mule works on this world to swill it, by faint response to drill it into loss. Flies flag of faith-defender: massacres all gods. Upholds all priesthoods: sets fire to their hands. Sings welcome to talent: dips it in holocaust. Prologue of spoilers since world began! Before world even, hiding in woodpile, hiding in seed of world before MA/FA, primal mistake *not* fortunate, sperm of our woes, sin saturate among hypotheses as to how world should be: foul worm of your own gut: how should love sing without you?

He has permission of morning to reach evening. Massively closed of late, doors of eternity open again: would *you* enter them and be lost? No, he prefers uncertain stay outside gigantic gates he knows to be for everyone alive: excepting him. He has begun to think she is a strange one to take a man crazy with stars into her house. But she can nurse her comfort: he's no astrologer. Distrusts each single one of those maddened lights. Sure none will ever actually come down, or stretch to reach him. Suddenly, remembers trains which started out from a known place, arrived another, stopped at a whole bunch in between. As long as they do that is all he'll ever ask or ever will require. Obsessional. He who wrote in passionate friendship a full year after meeting — but had not thought to send some sign between: what *do* you *do* with such unerring lovers?

"If only he'd slip off into the light of heaven" she had thought — but he would not. Here is a whole *noblesse* fiercely believing he has them by the root. Constrained to correspond with him each once a day; call him each once a week; lard him with gifts, honors, awards each once a month, take him to town for ice cream once a year: and, *no* he sits as lone as fossil locked in rock. With that degree of dryness you could not spark with matches however hard you tried. It is the flame-proof dryness of the pharaohs.

Then, he would remember palaces standing in their own sweat of summer light, roof sculptures turned this way and that — some talking at the void, some versing with each other, always one at least singing, a few avoiding others, a couple so completely self-en-wrapped, their steady gazes gashed fontanas into the cloth of heaven. From which new stars shone down. That fair rotunda famous throughout the world. Still, he dwells on in disbelief. Stars shine on down, ignoring palaces, preferring in cold wisdom a vernacular landscape. He is appalled at his fate: being a great believer — sometimes, he thinks, an only believer.

Project being kill bull and yet keep ears by public grace — bull's ears or public's, no one knew for sure. He waits, dressed in child's clothes for people to collect him: no suit of lights. Back then, had she not been as old as hills, opening to him, bone door, but all her lower parts surrounding it, springtime? Passionately, before going to fight, had breathed that new-mown grass, odor of long-dead leaves burnished to crimson, cherry, peach. Now he had wanted to be child again, received as such from birthday up — and there would be no break between that infancy, adolescence, death. Even gray-haired, they'd end by looking over this multicolored, satellite-surrounded planet. Innocently they came to be wedded here as if to receive a county. Miraculous, the county had gone to give itself to them — unalloyed.

But she burned. Where does it start, the sense you have abandoned meadow for trees? Plots stand erect now like sets of unmatchable particulars. They'll work themselves, threadbare you understand, into her story. The one you always love to hear. Who would survive to hear one reading only, he means *care* to survive? You would not give a nickel for a bone of hers, would you now — but what if bone stood up all by itself, named without waiting which way white beards would wag? And he, still sleeping there, under the anaesthetic.

Shadows moving behind the bone, named now, labeled on skeleton, purveying a relation-ship from bone to bone so that, at night, ah, you would lean, as if ready to hear, what: gossip? scandal? classified information? No: better than that, door after door opening into, not darkness no: dazzling light. Tale you had told her you would never write, let alone tell. Tale cannot be divulged at any cost, expensive as this morning is, soaking up light. As if light were about to fall for life out of production. And he now, like his father, sleeps the great sleep eternity, that had been laid to rest so recently, maggot-like, inside ground.

He wanted them to realize, at heart in this lost time, that he knew it was being lost. Multiply that by a given amount and you have his "stuff of several lost lives." You will never find their story: it is untold — therefore shall stay untellable. Without our presidential libraries, all is forsaken. Mind is adjusted without a single guarantee. Small twist of wire: it moves one incremental step, no trace of an experiment survives. Wire could have just as well twisted another way. There it hangs, in its own marvelous light, remote from anyone's control. What mind records bears unmistakable topographies of an old empire newly dismembered. My God! how he missed those long, fragrant lawns — and how those trees at their limits, where grass rose to inhale his light, called out for his return!

Father, Father, cried our maggot asleep in his wheelchair, you may come home now, all is forgiven. But his voice had meant "forgotten." Before its loss of song, no son had it afforded any sign of forgiveness. So, imperceptibly, he'd floated out of madness all encompassing into a sanity would gladden peoples' hearts until he died. Infinitesimally, he stood himself alone, grown giant suddenly in fine-grained daylight. He had poured himself into some blue, interline recess of his being — something, he'd thought, that no one, evermore, could take away from him. He no longer even cried at scenes of family reunion. After that, a prodigal never came home. There was no need to. He sent a mask instead. Stop spinning around that dark pit! He had heard and would try. Give away everything that you cannot recoup! He would be generous in his upbringing.

Far below contents of packets which came by mail each morning was "packet" itself. That it should have left its point of origin, traveled so far through frozen night — and *reached* him was all that counted. For that matter, packet could have been empty for all he cared. Once in his life, one packet had contained a book — "here, this was found for you" — and once, it had, by miracle, brought a star to his empty sky. Star belonging to him, he had thought for the balance of his existence, our father's star. Magnificent, belted, with sword and dog, star stood for recognition in splendid void of heaven. Devoid of all stars else. Had kept out all stars else. Stand by me! seemed to cry star. His eyes faltered. He had always needed the most angry scope to envisage anything at all.

Who had walked into immense and terrifying worlds of suffering never distant, to shut traps on all else. Walked with eyes turned inward so that inner face of eyes, when outward now, showed pitiable lust for friendship. Finesse required over one lifetime from such friendship known in advance no way attainable. And so small animal bedded down at heart, once and for all, losing all hope. You have done with such eyes? They could not swivel back into a world of suffering, immense and terrorist. On another side of this place into which he had entered, radical friendliness continued shining out of countenance: movement of welcome to an outer sea become primordial ocean of churned milk.

So that what had been done to those eyes was they were not to be met. From friend to friend had he not wandered, hearing the names (and their innate impossibility), wanting to push it, not pushing it (sojourns so short, so much to savor in such cities)? Among the line, gorging themselves at a buffet, why had this one, choosing a single slice of ham with ineffable meekness, precisely this one, this one alone, extracted such a flood of repressed weeping? An epilepsy among those inner eyes, as long as remembrance would last? Knowing almost all those who knew him, yet had he not continued never to meet? Borne in excruciating shyness his own cross? While both their signs had always shone together, in a full sky of unquenchable stars?

He would have saved a life, perhaps as well as may be, collated river with his own surmise, had he been able to dam that flow. How can it be sworn at this late date they never crossed among their birth streets? Oh, you that would have loved, but knew it not? So that river, rushing along its bridges, forever feeds his sea of churning milk. Let them take him from this city and he would die had been his primal oath. And he had flown with city, fluent in its clouds, who now flowed foul and fallen through its corpses. Shadow, breath shadow failing to reach you. Never to hold that hand. Not only those who have survived their lives have been deprived of them.

FIVE

Copyright Freedom

Arc 29 - 35

For several months, had seen himself in mirror old. One day, it had occurred to him, found himself young. Used to himself by now. From then on, went through life finger on lips with no more bleeding. Which is what it means to turn into a star. No more of that kneeling, in full carapace; face contorted, eyes awash with tears; bleeding fingers clenched in prayer descending slowly from bleeding teeth; whole body writhing inside the steadfast armor. No: clothed in light now, standing, frontal position, eyes steady, staring straight ahead. Small rivulet of blood at crown streaming downskull to forehead only. On way to nose and fingertip on lips. Likeness the cosmic messenger.

Had fame become greater in sunlight than his art? Always possible. Had men perhaps raped those creations? Sold them over and over so many times? That everyone, in knowing them by heart, now was losing faith. Losing virginity. As they acquired immeasurable value. The market place becoming tired of them. So that *seeing* them, *really seeing* them advancing on all this, would readily kill him? — Huge lassitude, big-breasted, welcoming, stove him to sleep like, bleeding the golden mind, to die among such fields. Meantime, had birds ever ceased flying from east to west this screen; from west to east all others? Baptism of spirit, shaken so, sharded, could only break one day, shatter of darkness.

Also no never, sounding among trees, rootwork of trees, footgrind of trunk — along all laboring paths, between all reaping garden beds, relived remembrance of what it was. Colossal wooden giants, arms thrashing winds, and thrashed by them. Like — not to be a star. Milled among beds, between cold sheets, ground by stone thighs, any and all, sawdust devoured by women. Sidelong glance of absolute refusal. Of absolute acceptance — though suspicious. His blare of effort, sisyphus at sun. Rolling sun that whole life, up hill, down dale, latter anyone of its days. Finally: sun rolling down the huge incline, those distant purple mountains, night flares in fading conflagrations, crushing at least this star in holocaust.

So that he could not stay still anywhere. Had nowhere to stand, nothing to stand on, nothing to stand on something with. Sit, sit on, nothing to sit on something with. Lie, lie on, nothing to lie on something with. Not knees, not ankles, elbows, wrists, chest, neck. How painful life become? Surpassing admiration that you nurse for major poets, painters, piano players, or even certain generals and striptease artists: you would have watched him fly, who could never take off, never land. Far into cloud he would go, peep out, soar back inside — as a glider does, high in the boundless over desert, sporting with thunderclouds, diamond hooked by desire to ivory and jet. Singing "my kingdom not being of this world, hey ho..." or so it sounded, but you stood on in expectation of "if not......*then what*" — and it never came.

It was where the singing of waterfalls could be heard by him alone that flight. Over clouds, mountains advanced, huge prows breasting mist, pointing back to oceans full of algae tall as trees. Beyond that green, palaces asleep among their gardens, drowned in unfathomed enthusiasm. Had he not laughed as he thought of them, sailing from moon to moon, peddling those prophecies of worlds to come? As world juggled with world throughout black space, confederations swam out of federations, sound let itself be organized at last in that unquenchable hymn? The one men had at one time baptized liberty?

But he who could by no means rise so far? What aim could he envisage, keep in sight, slave for, day, night, as "genius" used to do? Who was nothing, if not pure flight, flight so unqualified it would not ever weaken prose again. How to enjoy the lovely sapphire planet, the less it had those people in it his rope could swing to! And how it all began to seem like his alone after such black diaspora! A tree through mist was irresistible. What used to be a street, far, far below, gathered in welcome some shadow of his steps. A myriad houses to take his ease in! Had he not dreamed sometimes, moving through air, of beds beyond the sea, calm below breeze, on which he'd lie one day as kings once sat on thrones?

Take here one life. Wonders at nothing touching him in life what death will bring. Take here one death. At nothing reaching him in death what life has fashioned. Same deal. As if hardship were not enough in death: book lack, art lack, counterpoint lack. Harp without adequate talent? No way. Chance of a telling composition rating heavenly readings (or hellish)? Slim. Ah, but small worlds these guilds. And so reflesh. Small worlds can only breed small worlds: readers? listeners? viewers? Pah! paling fantasy! What *else* can poet be, when comes again, but poetry? Musician music, painter paint? So they will know, in future sinews, death's leverage. In their self-worship they'll know their finals in those previous times. But do not think winning is once again! These dice are *loaded.*

Climbing this mountain, swearing they will not dance. Known as "the men who will not dance." Arrive at summit. Look down mile upon mile of sheer. Present one leg, least-favored, to the drop — and throw themselves in the abyss. Land one leg broken. Rent cast: autograph, frame. Turn up at dance, apologetic; spend whole night leaning at a wall. Decorative, but foul of female principle: not asked again. How they are going to be damned for this, eternities, in tales of princess, pumpkin!

Those who, coming from somewhere, move down the line, forever lost, unable to return to somewhere. Those few, coming from nowhere, move down the line, unable to return, even to nowhere — exile from exile — how hard the point is! What then the *summa* of that desire: to find some deep original without the point? Two bodies wrestling, one male, one female : she striving to engulf one nipple to male mouth. He thrusting it away. Astonishment! What is eternity if not the love you never had at sunrise? Where ocean flourished in a million blossoms? Never to smile again but all through life to roar, with noise of most compulsive, battling waters?

It was no use trying to show humility; his truth would hang. If the vanquished live, sooner or late the victor deals with him — for he would have sinned in surviving his victor. Show forth the might to judge. Propose the guilt pertaining to the vanquished. Let right be done under objectivism. Or, in that secret cave of original breath (known as the heart of hearts among the heathen), hiss in the possibility of your own self-guilt. The question of technology has not abated. To be or not to be technologically guilty. Little they knew they'd not be poor for long! And if the world has grown communitarian so late that there be so much knowledge of something wrong with it...that it's impossible not to be metaphysical-guilty: what then is the past legend of metaphysical guilt?

Not making now. *Study* of making. Soci-o-logos. Which or which not to *klüngel*. Can he commodify? Can she commodify? Can you (sing.)? Can you (plur.)? They will commodify you for the sake of art: cut off your nipples; set your pits afire; cleave your skull in two; barbecue your sex. War to the waffle — a preuys on prussiandom: it all hangs out to be sold. Eau de Cologne; Pisse von Dusseldorf; Scheißeboutique von Stuttgart — sauced a la Nueva York, glazed with the Angels. Artist sells dealer; dealer puffs critic; critic rubs dealer right: tell me who you deal with, I'll suck both cock and nipple. Clemency waits to tell us what the kipper. Sally plays dumb while buggering the skipper. Is proto-fascist neo-fascist — or both plain fascist?

This year, we deem that City A will lead the market. Leal a deal A. Next year, let City B bag all A's artists and, the year after that, C buy both A and B. Nostalgic historicism litters every one but *you* might end conventional or mere particular. To fame or not to fame at cocktail parties, fifteen minutes or more: warhead to starboard is the angel of record. And how the ten percent above commission will cream all seven volumes of the catalogue. Jazz up the new; regild the old; bring round each statement in its turn to build the stall: steal a deal B and diddle with C — no ox covers no cow shipshapes us all. Futurians, heil and farewell, consumer tides return! Adore *das arme Ding!*

What can be seen from the left hand. No longer the vernacular road, no longer the political road, the way to the capital. Landscape as space deliberately created to speed up nature, query, to slow down nature, query. Shows man his shoulder for the role of time. Not of all earth: of one specific place to which road goes; not of earth wholly but one place only. Not the great city; not an *imperium* easy to find, easy to visualize over your all — but the small place: poor, tucked among motivations, mountains and valleys, hills, river sources, the smiles of flowers. A great mouth hidden, out of which you came; the only mouth, the one and only, smiles right across that wide horizon going from left to right of your bay window — what though that mouth repeats itself over the earth, smiles everblue from the whole universe?

Hearth; field; wildwood: three concentric circles leading you home. Beyond the given, consumerizing home, all wild — *horrida silva* — unusable, to which one never traveled, where the various gods displayed their awe. *Marge:* margin, exploitable forest, home of wild grass that the cattle may find change of fine pasture. Is *this* the place? To have no dead in the place; no roots; no children — only the mind roving like wind over the place: is this home's name? A place from which the bells are heard: that is a home — but bells are silent here; he does not hear them; he's never heard them outside *inmargination.* They're come to desert then: ocean of sand, all profit margins erased and buried, to be born grandsons, both for voice and lineage.

Waiting. Sun turns around the house. Still sitting, waiting. Sudden strikes window, floods in through window, floods over page. Sun doing all. Sun doing everything, they nothing. Classless society is here: they merely have it, no effort whatsoever. Now nothing happens. The threat is nothing happens — for a long time. Can depth not be achieved in nothing happens? That the not-happening spread out, like a vast sheet, fall inward, full of fish of nothing happens. World suddenly in place in the not happens. An absolute of nothing nothing happens. The absent of all buckets.

What and weather to make of time. To make of world. World silently at its preoccupations; yourself beside yourself at yours; beside yourself at winter, autumn, summer, spring. What can world say proves it approves of you — and what can you desire to say of it? That, somehow, world gently dances in tune, with the sense you have of it dancing — or walks, or even shambles, out of tune, with what you have of it, falling? Moods, like the colors you give to apples: certain as those, *your* mood, profoundly hearted at any given moment, gladdens the prophecy? Yes — but in those moods where there's no joy, where world collapses to everlasting: how then can you not fall, but hold to purposes: newsless, unaccessed, *uninformated.*

Out of the desperation, common, garden or wild, our daily bread, what cannot lift us? From that the which is what it is and ever seems to have been. (In brotherly love, when you went there, Top Gun's *name* did anyone know it? did anyone tell you?) If we'd reached peace just now, that invisible ocean, our will to rest...it's understandable. But it was reached far back in time, chock-full with whales cavorting, great fish to swallow us and take us to their easts — where our nomenclature, the only prophecy, could have been spoken to some purpose — and not left rotting here, among the vaselines, jellies and contraceptives. But to go moving on, go moving on for clarity alone!

These few, who kept repeating, re-occurring, re-manifesting. These few with will to move, although the word had stood to motionless, the sail lay disinvested! That were the souls of some lovehead men had only imagined, but *strongly* as if designed to last. As if that world had needed them and heralded their coming. White faces, born of sun, with yellow beards and curls, shored up again from dying out of eastern waters. All by itself, world having turned around, forgetting one day lost in the midst of days, leaping straight over ocean to beginners' beaches. Murdered, hearts clawed out. Nothing can save you now unlike salvation.

His hills and valleys stand about his outing. From century to century, looks up, cognizes fortune. Clear north wind day. Waters dream over all, sea both in sky and under sand — unperishing, uninterrupted fire. Sun shoulders shadow, slant falls across both pine and juniper. Out of silence, wisdom bats softly, always occult at the head of the eye, blinking among her foam of feathers. Tan feathers and the rising horns. If he forget both fire and origin of breath, he grounds among the hills and valleys. How stands this fortune he glares at day by day, unwilling to collapse into the deathful?

Absence of name, void as fields between stars. This place astonishing. Pure field. Mile upon mile of field (every conceivable direction) — plus up and down, plus center. The farthest place he'd ever come to. He did not know; he was not sure; he'd have to look for proof — but then again he might have found, might have discerned, the treasure island. That this perhaps at last, this might have been, the innermost, most immanent, core of his darkness. In the midst of which, with nothing round it for a thousand miles, they'd built a Center of Centralized Studies the like of which no one had ever seen. But, studying in which, he could not move at night a few suburban blocks down to his home.

Womb as restraining matter: flower of flower as such we are bound to, lining from which we float into this birth. Inside? Seed of itself, exciting him, slaking the soul out of enamorment which then can summon her and kneel her down before him. Petals distill a dew to fall from crown to root of darkness, then to flow up again to other petals at body's ultimate, most diminutive mouth. Where sun awaiting beggars the trick. Of she what has been eaten is a field of produce sown from her every pore. She drenches out his dew into the earth — and with it all attachment to the withered flower. Freedom! He'll copyright the thing so that it stays a secret, no fodder for the vain. Only their bees come alive, self-born of their own honey. Patrivore and Matrivore devour each other in showers of fine laughter.

SIX

THE PROFESSIONALS

ARC 36 - 42

ARC 36 : 90

So how was the man to know you hit the ball so far, so high, so universally, the home run ran along the rest of your life? Who had howled at the moon with the best of his buddies and wondered where all the golden arms had gone. Why his was common brass. Yet who, with brass, had hit the requisite hellslams to be counted on the hands of one arm (say thirty-five fingers) among the victories? Had he not stood with the public's triumphant air of players on their brows, signing each others' bats and balls right and left? Barked a few orders for a while to have them crowding round him — as if his voice had been platinum-plated in the ultimate ballpark of fame?

Naming them one by one in a numberless population, what else is this if not counting shells in the ocean or giving a name to each of the waves? So that it is done for the ever-greens at the bottom of the Sargassoes, for the eternals on the slopes of Everest, for the crown of light at the peak of the North Star, oh friends, the weariness! Feet bound in shoes of clay; arms in plaster casts; hands in elastic gloves draining the blood of its salt, year in year out — but had he not looked at himself in the mirror, saying just another little while, child of light, and there will be this homecoming to electricity!

To where she had kept the records. For no one better than she — have you seen those books? — knows the true score. The neatness of that handwriting? — no one so sharp as she to save victory stats! A mind like a municipal computer (with the brain of an angel pitcher) and no one dances? What though no other sees, no other witnesses — it is white, when it was black one time, dazzling where it was once obscure and the sun sets in a mist of glory as if it were impossible to drink the desert dry. It will take longer than for most, and that's it all.

He being dead, one can go into oneself indefinitely now. It is possible to enter that huge tomb without danger of superstition. And pray for miles. He had begun finding himself by the theft of a fountain pen. Which had been his by right — yet denied him for years. A calligrapher? Never! He was now way beyond all possible writing. The small, four-footed scribblers who dealt with holy scribing in normal times were exhausted at their own invisibility. Animal gods. However hard they came down, with four feet to the ground, their paws left no trace whatsoever. In fact, they were hardly calligraphers at all — left a long way behind the capital in a sort of small mist, extending hardly a city block in acreage. Though they thought of it as the flower of human empires, of course it lost its currency the very next day.

No — stolen pens had quite another purpose. They became ... ritual instruments: adamantine symbols of a cast-off power that lay in wait now, behind bush or tree, for the birds of ill-omen to pass. All governmental figures were in at last: scribal personae were up over 80% in about one thousandth thousandth of the era's duration. Available commissions were few as blades of grass in the forever now decrepit fields. It would come to be a race in future between the scripture folk and other quadruped endangered species as to which might outstay which in unforgiving radiance. Note that for the bipeds — all had been given up for aeons already. As to the birds and such: one mantis alone held up the fields to heaven.

And she as the retaining matter, womb of reality we are dead bound to, world of reality-concerns which never let one free for a single moment? What is there yet to do? Ha! if there were things to do, the world would never be stopped! Seed by itself, set free out of the womb of concept: before concept is *no* is-ness. Absence of name — void as the fields between star families inside our sight — perceivable after long intervals in the heart of the unnamed. We are dead gone now, be sure of it.

What then of those who climb out every day, as if their lives depended on that regularity? As if to fly were only repetition, day after day — as long as wrists could be kept supple, feet sharp at pedals — not fall, like an explosion, quartered by the sun, wax melting into blood distilled at the withering shoulders? Instead of thinking: oh, a day, a week, an interval like that — why would it not be good for thinking with: perfectionism, interrelationship of factors, a deeper understanding of your craft's mysteries? Is craft not like volcanos, requiring build-up before eruption, the husbanding of strength so that eruption signifies, to make a mark upon the world, so that men notice?

Put their days' flights up end to end. They have gone out into the stars by then. Much farther than the stars in fact: out into space. Their craft has grown. No more a plane but some unlikely ship by then — gigantic monster, flying like a city — out into novel worlds beyond where anyone has been, or any flying thing, beyond even the gods, however spaced (out of the race) they are by such great distances. No report of them. No one to sing their deeds: no fellow-poet, musician, orator or priest. They fly unknown out there: no one has ever seen them backing out. How satisfied they are — but for themselves alone, as if fair fame no longer counted, epic dead!

So she's asleep, Erato, who bore the name of poetry just now... Calliope, that muse of epic song... asleep on airport benches, awaiting their return? She must make sense of them. Somehow, contrive to tell their tale, take down some details so she may weave a story, perhaps some pictures for the illustrations. Through the loud blaring litany of dates and times she sleeps: arrivals and departures, enplanings and deplanings — but gathers only... those vacant clouds. No record of those flights, save in the pilots' minds and in their hearts bursting with pride. The art is saved, they think, the records set, signed and delivered by officialdom, branded into the canon once for all. There is no one to tell them no one's heard of them.

It has to be remembered it isn't personal. Mountains collapse; valleys retch up; sea heaves above the land; sky crashes into mountains: the whole world seems about to disappear into the milky way — that path into the cosmic web of galaxies — and everything to end once and for all. It isn't personal. Species go down the rain; forests disintegrate; rivers dry out; not a thing spawns: the planet is about to join the other colds out there. Society and culture both have failed mankind; mankind has failed its gods. It isn't personal.

Social Science first. We are too many; we cannot all get jobs; we cannot all be fortunate — or even loved to death. The nation's a catastrophe; the economy fetid; the politicians assholes. The cultural bureaucracy (especially) is now illiterate, so dumb and mind-forsaken it's near gone critical. It's nothing personal. Spouse leaves you; children abominate you; parents cut you off; friends no longer call — or even send a Christmas card. It's nothing personal. You're fired from every job you ever held and simultaneously. No one will ever hire you once again, give you commissions, send good things your way. You are as dead in a dying world as if your life had never been. And there's no resurrection. It's nothing personal.

Psychology next. No satisfaction from the dreamtime? Perhaps your mother failed you. Or your father. Perhaps you cannot get from others what you lost on them. Not a single friend in the whole universe — a true, blue, trusted friend to whom there's nothing can't be said? Perhaps you thought unduly you'd crushed your puppy's limbs, strangled your pet canary? You are as lousy as anything created. And so, at last, you reach the final wall; the wall so thick that nothing will go through it — except yourself as naked as you were at your own birth. It isn't personal. This side the world, that side the work: no path that can be lived on both the sides. In the world you die. Outside of it... you might just draw another breath. You go through, no?

ARC 40 : 92

It has to come in through the blood — you will agree. Not mind, sinews, or lymph — only the basic blood. Nought else will let it drown like that, drink it up like a blotter. It has to come in time and over, until it has consistency, coloration of blood. It has to move along the arteries, when requisitioned: automatic, without thought, talk, preparation. It has to be instant — the very split second need manifests itself, without question, consultation, argument. There is no time whatever for mistakes: a single one would be an unforgiving. Would leave you dead. One was seen coming in the other day: despite the wide way open before him, like arms held apart and accommodating, he landed short. Wheels crashed through wings: everything was totaled. What got him? We don't know.

Hands, feet and minds. Several minds. A first, obvious one. A second, dreamy one. A third (possibly up from dragons) to consult the void and always find an answer. For that matter: maybe you need... several hands, several feet — like an Asian god. All of it to move together in one move: an absolute co-ordination. The work must respond as if it were a ribbon, unfolding out before you in perfect harmony, bringing together all things clear: to be as clear as day inside the final knot.

Who lives with you has no hands to work with; no feet to run with; no eyes with which to weep. But moves *en adelante* like a watch, each moment's heart of gold. From it issues the blood of learning; back into it the blood of wisdom. Perpetually, you go out into exile and, just as often, you come back home. No other habitation possible: no half-way houses, no hotels. In the end, there is no other being: you have unlearned all the forgettable. Retaining only the great wall stretching as far as eye can see, and even way beyond what eye can see. Outside of which, there's no life possible, for it encompasses all you have absorbed. Outside vocation: nowhere, drained and bloodless.

Standing on the high mountain of her evidence, it became clear to us this was the only way we could survive our life. You had to suffer insurmountable problems: problems so overwhelming that life would think itself defeated over and time again. With the profoundest sense that in no otherwise would it be o.k. to continue — only the stark alternatives of death, insanity. *Only* thus would you work greatly. Without becoming fluid dynamicists of the human soul. *Only* thus would you be able to survive the volume dated with your century. As for her, "my work," she said, "is my link with time." She intended to survive her existence.

Perhaps the problem with where we live is that it is impossible to have such problems. The ones she had. Conditions are not absent: we have at our disposal the best possible help for ignorance, stupidity, *mensonge* of every kind. We are familiar with misunderstanding of every description; neglect of every stripe, benign and not; insult to body and to spirit; crimes of the most wretched omission, abandon to depression and suicidal thoughts; absolute zone-outs from alleged friends: the list could be extended ad infinitum. All the conditions for having the problems she had are here — but the problems are not. Why? What are the comforts which allow escape?

The moment she was born, everyone decided spontaneously she was to rank among professionals. She carried auras from the very start. Even as child, she only had to walk into a room for an absolute silence to descend. She was invested automatically with a fantastic glamor — for which she did not have to labor one single instant. Legend became her the moment she did anything. Men fell over themselves to win her, shot themselves many times over in her honor, taking only the slightest care to remain alive. That youth was one of the most beautiful ever conceived by any being: and all the time she was creating and adding to her fame. It was only much later that the terror descended.

In the middle of a peninsula (almost an island and surrounded by an immensity of sea), the land itself separated from a forest outback composed of the world's most ancient trees, stood a great city with an astronomical number of inhabitants in a scarcely lesser number of fine houses. The inhabitants, so taken up by their business that very little else ever entered their minds, would have forgotten the forests long ago and even the shape and name of the ancient trees — had it not been for one sky-piercing colossus standing in the very middle of the city. It had survived there, no one remembered why. This tree stood in a yard among some poorer, smaller houses in an historic *barrio* and was entirely surrounded by a wooden fence. The fence was low, looking a little crazed beside the giant — as if attempting to imprison a Goliath who could crush it any time he chose. Fortunately, trees are slow animals and do not move.

With people rushing and scuffling around following noses into daily business, little could have been wanted of them, in regard this tree, unless they were to pass within its immediate vicinity. Occasionally someone would stop there and gaze in wonder at what they had so utterly forgotten — but now recalled as if it were the object of their heart's sacred affections. Then you might see such a person approach the tree very slowly and become almost as slow as the tree itself — as if wishing to be attuned to its heartbeat. It would be part of their evolving awareness, however, that the small fence surrounded the giant. Observers noted with curiosity that this fence would be as difficult to climb as one a dozen times higher.

Those who succeeded in closing with the tree would embrace the huge trunk with a span as wide and close as their arms would permit, remaining there long whiles — as if in prayer or an even more intimate state. On nights when someone had achieved this union with the tree, the city would be regaled with an unearthly sound more beautiful than any music known, seeming to emanate from the tree, or its vicinity, but filling the whole sky above the city and stretching back, it was imagined, to the distant forest as well as round to the arm-weary ocean.

SEVEN

June Snow, Manchuria

Arc 43 - 49

City of the Long Spring they call it: interminable spring — some would not hesitate to say eternal. Where all wear grey and blue — not like the colored towns to north and south. Where history has died. Yet people lead dramatic lives in the interstices of time. Only existences seem slow to us when looked at from the wings. As if deadened from pain and put to sleep. Students asleep now. Talks, lectures, seminars, one to one interviews, over today. (We monologued. So endlessly: no one ever allowed the flight of but a question to meet us in mid-air.) We sleep on also, sold into sleep by theirs.

All words exhausted. All possibility of words. We have exhausted virtuality. But flung ourselves out of all windows dancing. Rained through their minds. And they are sleeping now through the long spring as if winter had never hidden bears on invisible mountains. While the young sleep, an early summer brings on the longest light. In its shadows, figures move through their paces as if, at any one, they'd turn to stone. Some standing stoned achieve it. Or move on wheels. Dreamers forget to touch the pedals, to go anywhere special, so sunk in dream. This empire once bought sleep as a condition, now sleeps it as effect.

High trees all over town snowing in this mid-June. Like cottonwoods back home. A timeless snow of birth again. What winter could not do, staining our lungs with coal. With no calligraphy save death. Mucus. Such weight of mucus on the town, such sloth of spit in gutters. So many lungs out at this writing. Snow warms now in mid-June. Promises, promises. Washes through light with silence. A dozen gentle gestures from the infinite. A dozen repertoires of moves alone. Dancers floating down street: you can see only air, not bodies. Stress of that light, wash over limbs — whatever weight to body loaned while breath still hungers.

Train on a summer Sunday. Poplars along the tracks waving their hair. As if whirling their heads round and round from the neck. Wind aiming south to a crimson city. From sleep, one increment moves down to rash excitement. Count shirts, skirts, bandannas, blown from grey to flowers, blue to flowers, some fashion found. Sunday in palace city. People explode, seeds from a pod, numberless multitudes. Crimson eateries, fierce jealousies of eating, hard labor jaws. Jealous of the whole week, perhaps whole year. Mouths run with grease — duck, pork, fish, capon, noodles. Garrulous onion, brotherly garlic, trade union leek. Rivers of beer. Topped off with ice-cream in fanfares of colors.

Move up imperial avenues lined with trees, taller than any others we can remember. If only they had not — for generations — trodden trees down for fields, tomb-trees excepted. North wind blows men along like homeless sparrows toward these crimson tombs made by an alien race. Which once ruled here, as if by blood. These dead took over space, created space, laid space out in their image until no fairer city stood for space than this, the city of the dead. Old trees — no longer wintering in June for their great age — so old men have forgotten long how they were planted: this race or gods now equally long dead?

Enclosed by boundaries, we follow their directions. Not ours. Can't stray as much as thumb or toe outside those boundaries. Stone elephants and other beasts lining the ways; fierce ministers with swords; sons of the royal blood — all motioning men's dreams this way and that, but only in accordance with cardinal directions. Caught in one net with the dead, men moved by emperors on sundays. Joy of wind's push on sundays: a wind which moves them more than they can move. Caught in the sun like flies held by a crimson spider with too many branches from which to weave a net.

Of all most anxious to move on, these the most backward. Leap they gave forward once leaving past behind, future could not be recognized if it were demonstrated. How they would like to fly, these fledglings! How their fearful parents strive to prevent it! Too many suicides that once! Tenderly we try to give them the world — or rather how to take a world — for no world can ever be given or received. Not make mistakes we made ourselves or complicate things beyond all measure. Exact velocity of take-off; flight itself; landing and the capacity to do this every time desired. But pushing feather into dark, beyond the light it of itself would bask in, not.

"And don't forget" we say, as they dream on at us. Dreaming away at the edge of our faces, asleep in the drop of our lips. Dreaming only the good and the desirable, not our poverty. "Too little may be bad / too much is *just* as bad, and maybe more so. We have the tendency to push the universe so far, we may distress its axis." While we, in our own dream, cannot rise from our sleep, lift giant bones from comfort. Fail to trim fat, curtail desire, break appetite toward disaster.

Stir under snow, no more than that, but stifled. Silence where engines usually roar. No single crack in even fields of sleep. These others above ground, crossing long avenues asleep. The whisper of their wheels our only sound. Wheels overwhelm us with their quietness: wheels hardly touching ground to move along it. Wheels still in the warm air, bringing each point round to an origin — without development. How calm the dreams in their equalities: none stands beyond another, or rides on out.

Answers our question with his silence. Staring ahead, wishing that time would pass. Would pass or vanish into altogether. Then, as you are about to think silence will never break, the question circles round his head, careens, stalls, dives, loops loops — glides back toward his mouth. Lands on his lip. Idles a while. He smiles. Repeats the question. And, as if shadow boxing, bends down to answer. Lifts secret from its box, examines it, turns it over his eyes, under his tongue, brings it right out before us, as if it were an answer. Stark, bright, *correct*- a first created thing in a new world!

But it is not the answer we had looked for. In our deep ignorance of such a universe. Of the potential depths below the smiling of another country. We had thought all asleep, all winter through, all summer too — at least until the summer snows divorced their trees. Knowing the answers, sure, but only dreaming them. We thought our thoughts might fairly dance together: but they could only pass like birds, in opposite directions, even at crest of day.

"And where are the imperial tombs in this fair province?" — "That's a State Secret." — "But, we had figured only bridges, stations, barracks, factories... all bureaucratic maps, charts, documents... from A to Z, were subject to this rule?" — "No, Sir. Look, Sir: the truth. We have been so bedeviled here since time began, even our country's name is a State Secret." Rain washes him out of our house into the dark. He goes back to his thoughts, deep in the city's pipes, to lead his mole's life under the trees' foundations. For him, his multitude alike, each tunnel has its feast and date.

Great cranes pace through our minds. White against clouds, black necks, red skull-caps. Loud across clouds, stalking horizons we cannot imagine. "You are narrow, you say — but *we* are only just… a tad wider than you: all men are fundamental" (draw lines at black-board center, then pacing to each end and drawing lines there, at the edges) "compared to full extent of possibility?" Cranes feed at both our sides behind the board. — "For twenty years, Sir, lived alone right here. Rehearsed for twenty years, Sir, your language night and day (no chance to practice); read the same books, Sir, time and again — half dozen books no more, white fathers' gift in the deep south long time ago…"

"Look! Let me recite you, in your own language, the proclamation your one-time emperor made to his soldiers on the field after his greatest victory." The emperor we had two hundred years ago! In our dark room, that classic proclamation rings out in our own language: we boggle at this unimaginable devotion! After, he sits in pride as if fulfilled — and decorated by our admirative sighs.

Later, inside the night, great engines puff toward the south (since we're so far inside the north you cannot go to any place but south). Engines labor far harder than any ever heard in our own land across the planet. We sleep out ancient battles in a foreign war-zone. "Joined fingers jab and take the eyes out from the enemy. Then knee comes up and pounds the wind out of his belly. Suffers. Bends double in his pain. Two fists whip round, white semi-circles, slam into his ears." Cranes in our dreams walk widely white like snow, majestic so.

Beating the bushes for their poems — cannot see them for leaves. We ask for birds. "Birds? Not seen a single bird since year began; since time began if we have not forgotten. That is: to measure time and name it... Parks? Hard to find now in this middle earth (trampled by hordes) — only where sentries keep men out, there plants can breathe. We come here to escape our life, mourn time gone by and absent friends: we have not seen our friends many a year. Our love has passed away (had passed away before our birth) — and we have never found her! How fragrant undiscovered poems, warm in their dens like cubs all the year long!"

What is this? Where are we? Where has our beautiful month gone so soon? In which we found all the good of this land. Snow falls down June. Entering noses, mouths, ears, passing through us it seems, silk-like, transparent. And, as so often, we see at peak of beauty: beauty is going, love is gone. "June snow behind us, ground free of drifts..." We say to them: "Allow us freshness, please! We know you will march through us — but for now: show us only the *beauty* of your home at last. All men sin the same sins!"

"We know your topic, heard a thousand times. Number and reign of quantity. No matter what protocol is: smother with zeros and production schedules. Our boredom doesn't count with you; your custom is to bore us. To stuff us: words or food, all for your honor. You will march through us soon and out beyond us. Sending out teachers for *us* to learn. For now, just leave us. We appreciate... we even honor you. But: bare yourselves a little! Patience! Unbend! Where are your birds?" (annihilated). "Your dogs?" (cooked out of town and country). "Your wilderness of trees?" (under the earth). — "Just snow behind us, ground free of drifts..."

Indoctrination class. "Have been successful on accounting of: follow the policy correct. Because the policy correct, we are success. Next month, new correct policy. Shall be success, and success signify: correct discovered. Great source of bliss for us: policy always. Follow correct on all occasions. Now please! give com-ment, cri-ti-cism, so that we always may align correct. Also proceed to the correction of: the four, five, six correct progressions. This is a humble place. There's far to go." — "We did not ask to come into this life. We do not ask to live it. When the time comes, we shall not ask to leave. Tell me: what have this life and we to do with one another?"

Emperor's word to people. "When in the state of doubt, attempt to stray from path. Place one foot forward to the north. If your foot move, but you do not, place one foot backward south. And again, east, and, again, west. Foot moves, but you do not: one foot to zenith, and, again, to nadir. Then try diagonals: south-east and west; north-west and east. If your foot move / you still do not, try other possible directions one by one. Then stand fast upright, absolutely still.

The flat-faced student records every word. Has been recording every word for months. Such chance will never come again: his teaching capital for a whole life. Speak fiercely? Rip his cord? Fling his recorder out the window? Our flat-faced student flattens anger just like everything. From three to two dimensions; two to one; from one to nameless pap his students will inherit whole life long. (The other students just as desperate: talking of books with not a book to read; deeper in cave than ever dragon is). One day he turns to us his pock-marked moon; tells us his many names he's had from foreigners. Real name however is: "Thanks Place of Always Spring."

EIGHT

TIBET

ARC 50 - 56

Sure there must be a place from where you can depart. From where you go into your head toward that other place. That other place in which the where and when are made. In which you spend most of your life pursuing where and when. In which all those you know — almost without exception — are desperately lost. Or where they hardly know, or you, that all are lost. Or that this place, so like it seems not other, is yet indeed the same as the departure place. There stands the wheel of heaven. Its multitude of mansions between each of its spokes. There you go up or down accordingly. Also you never move.

And our eyes are so blind, the why rattles its cages like a raucous bird to so many a why. If eyes could see, there would be no why — only assent. Up we go into the mountains — feet accumulate by thousands; breath comes short on short; just tying up a shoelace you collapse from great heights. Up there the prayer-flags slap birdless air, songless altitude. Though there is always a raven to croak what seems the time and chat you up with some small prophecy. Silently you look around for your ram caught in his thicket. But the thorn holds you — no horn visible.

Eyes of turquoise water far down among the valleys look up at you in wonder. You wonder back. The rivers move between valley and valley among mountain boxes. She of all compassion with all her hosts: streams from your fingernails. The where, the when, the why carried toward the sea — far off and more besides in yet another country. Souls in our mouths locked in by these rough roads remind us that we have no place to go. Except out of the place of where and when. Back to that place from which we had departed: should not all travel be immediate return?

Gone away. Far away. Gone further: "beyonded". Beyond all borders — known, unknown; mapped and unmapped — beyond all possibility of earth (or fire, air, water) yet still retained, still grounded. But *elevated:* here roof of world, you high dominion, settled in snow for our salvation. In that pure white is no known basis, but combination of all elements, colors, determinations. Met with on roof of world, dark-wine clad men, loud sung, loud prayed, loud gonged, loud trumpeted, loud chanted. Noise of the thousand persecuted things — faith now their anchor.

You of a thousand eyes, sweet white sixteen and green, as the first thought of this conversion. Where snows abound, you fell from boundless skies, star with a thousand arms, all things enfolded. The highest sky we never measured, impossible to hold in one stray thought — as all thoughts stray. Though holding it in charity — toward all beings — toward the happiness of all and none to suffering: gone well beyonded, where hand nor heart can bring her down — but thought alone brings her about and tempts her, sweet light of our prime orient.

Out of my gut unwilling to this fray, out of my heart most tediously I bring her. Over. Over again, or say, day one by day. Faith always deliquescing. To bring her day by day without a shade of help from any faith she nurtures. To plunge, continue plunging: though air deny the satisfaction of a death in water, felt glistening around you. Air is but air and marks not. To die in air our heavy bodies fall but cannot tell the living from the dead. As in some forms of sleep so light only the trace of dream can tell from waking. Just so she sleeps among the snows — to let us all recover.

Stars over desert falling, on A., now Q. Question of borders called the holy country's: what once was A. today called Q. — which now is a foreign empire's. Night in a sleeper, watch out of window (train gliding over desert), lodestar Great Dipper over desert which echoes desert under home. Freeze in this foreign air. But love falls with a thousand eyes over our faces, warms them to life, eyes looking out at framed and captured stars. Soon, snow on sand rises to sky, rocks pray: we soar above a thousand mountains, bless our wives' star, give birth to rivers, watering the world.

Extension into K. as well as Q.: traces of ancient holy universe, now near extinguished. Mingling of peoples, faiths, texts, allegiances: who friends this world, who foes it? Tan ground builds up tan walls, tan dwellings. Out of such dwellings rise rich earth colors: ochre walls, dark sepia thatch, black ring right near the top — black on white deer and wheel of discourse — dark ruling over tan. Dark into sky as gold-rise: keys, conches, pinnacles, gold into sky the bluer for them.

Magenta, wine, profound cerise: men moving among walls, celibate, tending to tasks, to water. Tantra. Black turbans, red skirts, white torso wraps, ruled bright vermilion. Tantra: to unravel. To seize moneyless land and make it gold. Young faces but just now borrowed from sin. Old seen-it-all teachers babbling round us. Dark bowels of the buildings: walls pin you to the knees of gods; steep stairs ascending ever upward — galleries, chapels, walkways, rooms within rooms, corridors, labyrinths, all in the smell of burning juniper. Gardens of inner light within the darkness. The crowdedness. No nook or cranny left unfilled, patria positiva. All these things; all these things. Work toward up, less intrinsic existence. Dreams resounding. Dreams dreamt by a dream, itself a dream.

City born in a prayer, set down by prayer, built up by fervor; conceived in meditations, born out of meditations; all favored corners defined by presence: this cave, another tree (beneath), that base of hill, all shrines and chapels — whole capital made of a king's desire that love should rule the world. All men striving to happiness, avoiding misery — say it over and over as you sight each man; leave not a *single* one untouched by this projection — you care and holy cities rise in each continuum, peopled by saved co-humans.

The great king's dream: cave walls coming alive with the illuminati — spot here, spot there acquiring definition, takes on a figure gradually, becomes the savior A or B or C among the thousand saviors manifest on walls. Disciple holds the sun at his arm's length upsky while the great king dreams on. Soon cave is world, oven of candle heat and incense smoke, breathless with color. No faith ever on earth so colorful. Through narrow corridors circumambulate, drawn here by the king's dream, pinned to the walls by other pilgrims, feed butter into butter, sink foreheads into gold, leave currency and coin stuck in the butter, rub hands along the sacred rocks, self-emanate. Tidal waves of human smile. Earnest gaze, unsmiling, met with smile, breaks into smile.

In yet another place, king founds a nunnery close to his dream, then moves the river waters further from their bounds lest nunnery should drown. Whole site will move about at the king's bid: building topography of the power city. Outside, a greater sea pounds at the human town: sea of desire unsatisfied, hatred unslaked, revenge nursed over aeons. Sea enters gates, drowns men and temples, laps at the very heaven made of brick and stone your king raised in his dream, let others build. City becomes museum of itself, still hot with enough splendors to satisfy your dream. Dreamed since the age of childhood and the great explorers.

Between huge mountain walls: valleys, fields, irrigations. Perspectives vast, scouring across the plains. Far distant views of mountain villages — fists, knees of green tucked among foothills. Fire smokes at evening. Circles of animals in a mist grazing: everything infinitely distant. "Pure" nature — *our* west. Small human figures wandering with cattle in this vast, from nothingness to nothing, void to void. Problem of *doing* all the day in our frail minds: how *can* this simple life be led as we think leading?

Prayer-flag trees on buildings at four corners: sky/cloud/fire/water/earth. Order of colors constant. On animals, flags pinned to shaggy sides. The beasts so coated: heads and tails the same unless the horn be showing. In field, stone upon stone in very small (invisible sometimes) markedly heaps. *Any* high spot increased by such additions and, at the highest (mountain pass, tall peak), stone upon stone as who would reach to claw all human records from the sky. Unto him that hath shall be added but: woe to him that hath.

The record kept, quite clearly that, stone upon stone to heaven. Do those most haunted by impermanence keep records most? How come the crowded stone on stone of these (image on image, portrait on portrait, lineage on lineage, numbered all) where others, in the same degree of faith, clear space so clean? He that is clothed but with the sun; clothed but with light, and sees all passing like a cloud of gnats, dissolving in the noonday — he can be said to clothe himself, be clothed with the great armor. What think you, X? You, Y? He, Z? — A play of shadows among ribs of dream, dreamed by a shadow in a foreign field. Sun sets and drinks this draft into our memory.

Police car screaming along garden walls as we come out. Bikes of ancient vintage — with sidecar — soldier on bike, prisoner in sidecar, hands over face. Then, truck with standing prisoners, two soldiers each. Then, truck with soldiers loud with teeth, brandishing guns. Then, several more cars exhibiting soldiers in varying postures and positions. We have been here before on the way to death. This is a story advertising death. Whole city knows it. On way to death: pistol at neck in some suburban field close to the city. So the whole city knows it, with the red tick mark later on the poster. "An end to incarnation?" said the monkey king. "No," said the sage, "a passage."

Cold over heart. Green uniforms turning to grey, then black, reincarnate. A fleshing backward. Another city, occupied. Invader army, dressed in black, red slash at elbow. Collaborators everywhere and no sharp means to spot them. Army, clear out of bounds in this beloved city, walks backward too. Against the tide of circumambulation, soldiers walk back toward the start, undoing their own progress, mock the locals. Beasts taken out. Birds. People. Lumber taken out. Shrines. Temples. Treasure. Everything despoiled. But human tide sways on, evergreen smiling. The tenderness of human tides!

Sixty foot images smile down impassively; sixty foot reliquaries embalm the smile forever. Pass beyond memory of man: this star of human nature cannot fail. We are reached; recognized; embraced; encouraged. God eyes are vacant looking far afield. Below them, smiles mirror human tides and give back smiles. Worship rewards these smiles; the self-reward — before eyes close on sundered benefits. Buy me! Purchase me! Lord of deep heaven; Lady of deeper sea, embrace me in your arms and take me to you! Gold in the darkness splinters; lips force a smile. Profoundest music takes us in abreast a tide of silence.

Closest approximation of uncertainty. In all its glorious rags and banners. To certainty as you believe it may be. With its one gold horn, pointing, one would presume. Presumably upward one would presume. This exhibited to, in manner soft or hard, bowing toward whoever may hold a certainty. That certainty propounded by the teacher. Never explained however; never *fully* explained — and thus for which there is no absolute, no gilt-edged guarantee. That to it can apply, or to you be applied. Your close approximation to a truth untold, unnumbered, colorless, unvoiceable. Which no one can scale and no one can fathom. No one can tell to be absolute truth.

Watch battery gives out. Watchless at dawn to tell the time by. Buy a new watch — old watch starts up again. Now: one worn at each wrist, set to different worlds. Left our own time whatever; right, their own time — and we go out between the landscape and the sea; they right; we left (with the sea) and which has certainty? Small island down below, way out at sea, surf-washed, is neither land, nor sea — whose is it then for certain? Stars now, over the desert, to echo one's own home. Sand: is it land... or sea, understanding the sea? Look how it deliquesces wherever it may flow — without an origin, without an end.

Love with a thousand eyes falls over ours, warming our faces, bringing them to life — faces to life frozen in foreign air. Love as a certainty without desire, gone far across to the beyonded. Great countries now conversing with each other as we prepare to move into the heartland. Today, a quantum leap at space, above all peaks — where love surveys the earth in all her kindness. Now love will guide to harbor safely, where we can bow in tune to the uttermost masters. Here congregate our stars' eternal recognitions. Shires of blue splendor shine where all compassion strikes. From a myriad planets — at the body of wisdom.

NINE

JUNE SNOW, THE SILK ROAD

ARC 57 - 63

The bone is seen. Having seen the bone makes all flesh seem more closely kin. All color drains from flesh toward the white, or colorless, neutral, unmarked by race or grace. There is no difference now that can be spoken of. Monotony. The similarity of all things born will kill you. What else can cause delight but searching for the flesh which still surprises, an only flesh, for sure, among all flesh? Avoid all else since weariness itself wearies of itself. Delight is all still links you to the ocean of beauty. Without whose wave we could not move at all — or break the patterns. Perhaps the patterns blame you when you cannot break them. Perhaps your uniforms are to be blamed, unfriendly as they are to color. Where do you look in all these sands for sainthood?

Perhaps solution lies in the only solution which takes not one into account but great heaps of ones. In which you have no place at all. Or the place of an ant in an ant hill barely. Choice after all is a personal right of the rich, the beautiful, the privileged only. But you must be sent where you are sent; accept a place and life alone or one and only, a place and life devoid of any motion. Picture merciless eyes measuring you, dispensing life to you, hard and unsmiling! Picture the motionless when they discover where they are to go before there is no going. Or: after which gone, then there is no more going!

A whole existence in one impersonal decision. Some sit without moving in a soundless storm. Some collapse forward, as if immobilized by electric hammers. She dissolved only to hysterical laughter. Laughing, she walked in circles for a lifetime of hours. Flesh falling off her as if clothes were falling — clothes having fallen first — for they judge you naked. She then walked up the mount of sand surrounding the city, walking for hours alone with the sand moving, making no progress up the mountain. She then moved back to where she'd started, staying still along three nights of three whole days. Following which, you can only discover an eternal acceptance, the sight of one friend only once in a while — after years of no one, nothing, the new life only.

A move from both ends of the earth. Slow progress toward aims unreadable. Insoluble debates — yet moving you, fraction by faction, inch by inch, forth to each other. Had been impossible, that whole month long, to breathe with any peace of mind. Because, each place you turned, needles were poised to enter you. High dread of needles, since infancy, brought you to bed year after year. Had been impossible to void body or soul of pain become the silken tissue of every day. Though you were told this pain would end all pain, this war all wars — and there would be a final sufferance. Now (sudden thaw), gold tides loosed over hills, hills drowned in valleys: all things made equal. Except the poor, eternal poor, stared down all time with deathless curiosity.

Now, suddenly, you move in this direction and — no needles, here, no needles, and neither gate nor wall. Intelligence illumines the great land; banners crack in the wind, arguing victory; hope (that grinds you deeper into earth than misery) lifts you a moment to summer skies. You can explain, without pre-judgement; acknowledge they know best — your students — what is best for them; concede a point or two; break under common knowledge; understand. They can be looked at, in the eyes and in the teeth. They can be held mature. You can move westward now through both your wests. And feel them move you, east.

As in a vision, through the sands, where sand seems to encounter sky, is she water? Is that body waving through grey and blue, unknowing a straight line, all ripples, sometimes waves, is that now human, animal, or dream? Is she, far off in future, sum of rest? Home-coming to the silent fanfares, deepest triumphs, music profound none needs to play, it sounds so far into the strata of the soul? Is this the single, only, picture now, the one representation of the human? So that they cannot ever talk of him again — but only her? Where, through the blue and gold, all the world's treasures crossed diameters of space, was this the dancer now uniting empires that never had known peace from war in centuries?

Song of the price of knowledge. Who had been in the dark for months on end, a dark of other minds. Starved. Stunted. Deprived of longing even. Joy of a passage from that blurred world, donning the glasses we are always losing: words stand out sharply, ready to labor, already singing on their pages! Now face to face, riding wide-bodied carriages instead of mustangs, taking twenty four hours to cross the desert instead of two thick years — and yet this desert takes us in as if we still spilled guts to get us empire. Uphol-stery all white, bridal intensity, huge linen beds to lie in as if protected. Our lives written on sand within each other's sight. Looking way out over the desert: the distant figure of a human, standing pin.

Is he the great explorer returning to be branded? A thief of knowledge by those (he might believe) sang, loved and honored him for his discoveries *on their behalf!* His pages num-berless as this dead sea's sands; his decorations quite as lavish. Can the desert begin at ten of eight precisely after that spacious river dividing north from south? Will he go through like Moses? The golden sea branch out into a tree of rivers? Are those our camels in a rift at eight o' three? Before our preparation, we are sucked in. Travel tries most right here for the *serious person*. Plunged in the golden sea to turn it sunset orange, learning not yet exhausted — yet decisions taken. Grossly we are determined now without recourse.

Sitting across from me, our time, no longer young, is mis-identified. Where is this year and will it fill a book? Across her knees, lying like a small child in an imagination. We played the game of hands at our first meeting, hands dancing round each other like four birds — on air as light as sunshine. Never alight: except at last with rage for that close knowledge, the sudden overtaking. And every time like this: a day will pass, a week, a month, a year — some interval for sure — but then it will begin again, the lovable beginning. How fortunate! To say to an old angel with a man's old lips: how I did love thee when we rode those trains! And ever since — as if all days were dawns, were mornings only!

Atrocious desert. Salt. Interminable trains run through great channels of white fire, ardent in sunlight. Even the sand has given way to salt: no animals, no humans, no whatsoever life. Two yesterdays ago: travel along a valley paradise where men had tried, above a desiccated stream, to carve their mountains out into the image of heaven. Details of heaven simile all carved: details make anyone believe heaven exists. Enough theology in stone to learn for lifetimes: no stone of it could ever be exhausted. No angel that could not be fitted onto one such stone. In two tomorrows, finding the water. Boating for hours on the wide river — so wide it was a lake — coming through mountains taller than genuine heaven.

Once at the destination, prevented from such sights by rabble legions of gatekeepers. The living rock locked behind glass and every heaven window covered with iron bars. In many places, this rabble said, it was too dangerous to climb the stairs. Wood would give way, even the angels moved roped round the waist. What is this heaven where you need a rope? A man has died here who did not want for heaven. Admirers came from everywhere, carrying flowers — white flowers to be hung from every bush as if salt snow had fallen on the sheen of summer. The gods disliked this show of love. Blood flowed under the flowers flooding huge floors of earth. On the great flag of blood hooding the sky, white flowers floated, orphaned of heaven.

Into the heart of heaven angel-winged she moves and angels follow her upslope as if they owned her. Where is there known such iridescence on the wing as she will demonstrate with all her butterflies? From the salt plain, thirst quenched a breath ago, they rise, their wings over her wings, scales over feathers, the sun finding the jewelry to play with — unbeknown hereto.

In the blue morning, hills on fire. Blue poppies shining through the fire, waking from under emerald hoods. By noon, the sun has drunk the hills, spits out bleached bones. Colors drained out of hills like blood out of a body. We come to shadows: rows of infant trees growing through veins of water. Green hands reach out like vines to grasp round everything alive and start to cup the moisture. In their cool arbors, children with raisin eyes gaze questions at us with one clear formula: are you not of the grape blood, same as ours, not slaves like us to the same god, same hungry sun and its black heart? Seeds of the great migration covering the earth, devouring thrones and dominations in your path until we reached that gate, the ultimate, that not even the prophets could go through?

What shall we make of those who turned to fire when that white fire for years has turned to ashes? Must they be honored for the old fire's sake, the white fire for the red? Through all our populations, anaemia spreads, aphasia also: hymns turn to lamentations under every arbor; smiles burn to blood, blood pales to tears in every rug and carpet; the wine runs milk, milk churns to lava, the grape is petrified, the fig dissolves, the childrens' eyes rot out, their foreheads shrink, there is no way to count the generations, fulfill the lineages, pacify the tribes.

Love darts with swords in her eyes among the poplars, clashing with mine. But I wear a hat the color of sky and dragon scales culled from the mountain torrents: so you may remember the waters hailed downhill to feed and wine us in the name of joy. Ah struggle! Above this red heart of the mountain chains ringing the village, late evening before dark, goddess unveiling — immense white mountain rises from red hills. Why once we saw it after many days (in worshipful attendance on her temple there) once only eyes beheld its crest far higher than expected, eyes lying yet but barely at horizon level! Who tells the difference now between the rise and set? Covered with her ice armor to cool the world down here.

A million crickets sing over town as we come in. Waves of sound drowning out the houses. In rage at the sun's heat: the houses waver and desist. Question of moment over and over: is moment speaking or unspeakable? Center of town: parade ground, pit, abyss, all soldiers broken into it — as if the town had fallen from their singing. On the circumference: veins of old town, along which flowed in from the west those old time caravans bartered for food and sleep. If you were to throw a bale of silk vectored back east, it would go ten ten thousand times around a woman's waist. We prefer south. Devoured by ants on every path to heaven, the mountains throw us back, earth-waves refusing passage. We bleed camellias in anticipation of a further south.

Now pleasure's been extinguished in our time. "My heart flies like a bird back to old courtyards, lives birdlike in a cage seen through a portico, with roses opening in darkness, letting my blood flow through. Between oasis and the desert in a singing noon, I want the soft green courts; worn, painted woods; delicate marble landscapes; calligraphies curling around the tongue, carved and covered with petals. Give us the loveliness of well-watered things, for this I'll barter birdhood willingly. I'll hide, never begging, never asking questions, grey dog inside the shadows along walls."

Child of the golden hills — who is aware now of some such bitter passage through this life? Of the hill towns they've made a modern city, broad avenues, lascivious gardens. Deep in the empty heart, where the palace was, there is a suasion of flowers as if to say: look you this city of all cities still perpetuates the passive magic of your infancy. To listen, gaze, take in, distill — and not to move, not to discriminate! Among the blue anonymous (that nameless ocean of blue slaves) from time to time a human flower from the lost world erupts, flies petals, ribbons, flags. Nothing on earth was ever clothed in such riddling beauty. Thanks to the earth for it: the gods survived. In the spring air of summer she smiles at us.

A country with nothing but people and no country. Land eaten up by locusts: however huge, all eaten up. As if they'd never realized it was them devouring: mere swallowed live by daily increase. Now there's only one place left of the whole domain. Island in western sea, mountain on island, road around mountain, stone road up into heaven. Road snakes so high it enters cloud, so narrows only child can pass through hole in cliff like thread through needle's eye. To climb up to the golden demon's shrine along a path in rock (for one creature per year to walk and meditate) five hundred squirm along the rock per day, hell bent on getting through.

When shall we all be capable of coming up again, anxious for life, thinking what passage into void can mean, passage from void to void, when shall just anyone come back this way again, be wanting to? Show us our fates, lords of this universe, that we may sleep those two more hours we need morning by morning! Mist thickening, rain coming down, covering mountain, whole people pressed up path head to the needle's eye, much thicker than a child. People rope thick, ravenous thread. As they come into cloud, trying to press together, become as thin as wafer in the press, slide into ultimate where demons reign. They stand on nothing, trying to pass over air.

Grey crowds, with flecks of blue and olive, melt into sidewalks. Far on the avenue, a giantess twice tall as all the rest towers toward us. Bronze head completely shaven, figure all muscle, red shirt flown by the mountain wind, dust cloud round waist sheathing silver sword, black leather boots outfitting her and red box hat rimmed with ferocious fur. How can I follow her who looks at us as we would look at her if we had pride enough to walk out of the sea — instead of swimming for existence? Many a portrait taken: this one glides over effort like a goddess. Unreachable will kill us, grinding our bones to dust. She walks ahead, back turned to us, leaving a wakeless solitude no one can breathe. Her counterpart in black (man studded silver like a sky with stars) will manifest tomorrow. Somewhere among her hills, still standing when the demon's mountains have collapsed, she stalks her homeland snows, the last red flag.

TEN

Surviving The Life

Arc 64 - 70

A wall to go through as a matter of course. No discussion, ever, of the wall. No proto-knowledge, except in theory — which doesn't count now. At the most, a notion that a wall might stand as a good metaphor. For what should be gone through — if any "going through" there is. Nothing dramatic. No particular prep, just a whole lifetime. No ritual for sure: no pageants, flags, fine uniforms, no celebrations of any kind, no witnesses. To what should there be witness? No perception of anything special taking place as you entered the wall, stayed in it perhaps for some fraction of a microsecond — and went through. No sensation at all. As if anything that could be said of going through the wall would only be sayable — not before, or during, but only *afterward*.

Comfort of being on the other side. Immediate comfortable feeling — though not a cause to that identifiable. No way whatever of defining feeling any the more precisely. Simply: *comfortable*. As if everything on "this" side of the wall — the one you are no longer on — were done with. Ended. Or consummated. Indeed consumed. Hard to know surely. But: continuity of feeling good. Something "you sure can live-with," even *enjoy* the "live-with." Enjoy your flight, enjoy your day, enjoy your life! Do *please* enjoy your life! Something — even — in which you can *exist. Where* you can live. More: where you can believe another life. Or, if you like, survive your previous life. The one on "this" side of the wall. You try the words inside your mouth and they sit well: "I am surviving my life."

"At this point in time," you are looking for your "she." The one who has always lived in this position. Who always comes up in this (third) stanza — so often, let's be honest — that you've been criticized. Smacks of sexism it seems. Will not wash these days. Not "pol-correct," as they are wont to say. You pass. You are a biomale and likely to remain so — whatever the investigations. Always been natural for you to be transported. Body and soul toward the female — and sing during the transportation. Most likely to remain the case. But the "she" is not here. Not externally to you at any rate. If not outside, then inside? Check it in. Curious survival!

A matter of the greatest possible simplicity. Not a question of mind/no mind — intelligent, discriminant, or not. Nor one of hierarchy. Who will tell when a flower ripens into a fruit? Many! Who will tell *exactly* when a fruit is about to fall to ground? No one! Never that *exact* moment. That *exact* circumstance of wind or weather. Everyone else, at this point, sits at the base of the tree. It is a little uncomfortable: the earth is wet with someone's hair being wrung out. Floods issuing from that dark river of hair, celebrating an absence. Speculation begins, soon is rife. It was achieved this way, that, the other. Through deeds in this or other lives. Accumulated merits. Wide generosities, some unheard of to date. Through powers of brain or brawn, spirit or wind, or grace bestowed from something, someone greater.

The wall's component stones lie roundabout. They are examined for evidence: someone's gone through. Stone remains stone. Birds open up for signatures, patterns of the impossible. Books are consulted, encyclopedias drained by the ranking scholars. Sages come out of every corner, province, state of the universe — some green with anger, some gold with equanimity. The prophecies are scanned — from the era's beginning — to look for correspondences. Noise, noise and hubbub, ever louder. Babel rises over and over, falls down a thousand times. Simply asleep among your trees, there on the other side, you sleep with all your sins upon you, in no way carried into grace, yet satisfied.

You remember marriage. The comings together, fallings apart, joinings, copulations, extasies... also the profound sadnesses, *"la chair est triste, hélas, et j'ai lu tous les livres."* You recall the sweetness of its triumphs; its quiet resolutions — as one of you moves slowly through the other's vision, not even knowing they are seen and cherished. But loss and treachery as well imprint upon you, lead-lode drawn through your life: there's no repose from them, not a single moment. *Here,* on the other side, four lips move through your lips; four ears hear the same music, sweet or sad. The lovely calm some sang descends on all you do, certain it's been agreed forever. All noise outside recedes, irrelevant. All is the garden cooled by its wine and honey.

The demons, naturally, will not let go. The further you are on the other side, the fiercer persecution. They do not come with lovely nudes, alas! Only with the foul kind of slime verminitude produces, lowest on register, most inferior breed: and it is *these* that you are cleared to lust for. You know them by heart: you suffered them all your life. They are those in the game who will never win. Yet who persist year after year, despite all evidence. Therefore — they run things, make sure *you* cannot win, sure *your* persistence, however close to the eternal, can never triumph. No card in this foul pack for queen success. It is arranged so that there is no answer, call back, revenge — however patient you will ever be. Voice: you will never have it.

They cleave to figuring the *quantitas* of your disaster. Of course, they magnify it to enjoy it more. It is, at the bitter end, all they can own. Your adamant is that *they* know all this about themselves, suffer in silence in their golden clothes, certain they will be ashes when your ash is gold. Too late for you of course. For this especial life. But now you know you're in another life. So this can hardly matter.

You would willingly deal with a beautiful nude if she could be their wife. One wife for the whole lot: all they deserve. You could expend your last imaginings on her, surmount *that* obstacle. Eating her shit, drinking her piss and blood, breathing her breath, liberate that horror! Grant her, in one last thrust, the unimagined pleasure — and then withdraw it. Also the god of vengeance said their lord, smiling friendly. Demiurge of what? Of all that needs a punishment and will not understand it. Revenge — and will not feel it. Annihila-tion — and will survive it. The residue of evil, that final rattle. Long, endless long, snake homes to underworld, hides under rock. You keep a wary eye on it from your expensive vantage. Her being rises steadfast as it always was. Triumphs among her ruins.

For him who struggles whole lives through and never rests. Though late beginner, aged on meeting with the kingdom, though most about to die just when salvation dawns, that farthest father of a western wall, where sons of every manner can go down and where sweet mother ever points the way, that is the nation he desired. *"An end is come, the end is come; it watcheth for thy health of mind, behold it is come. The morning is come unto thee,"* o thou poor citizen! *Thou* art the nation wedded, citizen, none else, no other voice, o my poor friend, my fathermotherland! So do I dream of thee, on that far side of any wall, having become there in my very song, that manner consecrated.

Who then had brought himself to the edge of drowning in that sand, of choking in that river, where all the good and all the evil he had done had come to similar conclusion: that it was all of one cloth, of the one water, like thread to thread, like drop to drop — had anyone committed to a pleasant end, a lovingkind conclusion? Had it ever been said that love would be returned, another cheek returned, that simply on account of love, you would be loved as well? Nonesuch and nonpareil. There on the grave it could be read, graved on the tombstone out of rock and marble: *"You who are radiant, look down on my desire, the sweet boy of my youth, no longer desolate, for he is come back home"* and the dove's voice is heard, like liquid honey running on the land! And answer right below: the love I offered is *not* returned, I die alone a multitude.

Ah she was young, the country, the sweet land, with laugh like music in throat's depth, a smile in every word as it might issue — or merely be suspended right behind her eyes! How other nations had grown old and sorrowed and then died — for loss of empire, dried up for lack of oceans to reconquer — but she, the everyoung, rebuilt herself anew, in every epoch, in every pore, rose artery and vein. Had she not been desired, clung to as the embodiment of the great tongue, *the voice:* had ruthless man not taken her to wife who owned the land she burnished — and all its sounds? *All* given up for her, *all* sacrificed, as much as half a life thrown down the drains of the old world to gather up the new! And now the price: to rot on your own altar, with not a bird in sight to devour your guts!

We were the antidote to time! Through the vast window back of our heads, the sacred mountain shone, covered with snow on the west side, the side of mourning. Black mourning turned to white rejoicing, as if a bride were coming home. Fortunate, fortunate sons are we of the great country, of the great sky. This morning, sharp, repeated raptor's cries tore the fine air to ribbons: we knew they had returned to hunt our forests. All was as still as hope, the sky unmoving through (the clouds immobile), a window in a backdrop to a movie poorly done. While hero hunted through the universe his rainbow's end, we stayed at home and ruled the empire. Massive, the emperor stood, joined to the empress; sun married moon inside the mountain.

From the romantic to the classic to the romantic to the classic... to the romantic: there is no end to it. Behind the queen of beauty for whom a war of worlds had burned, there stood another queen — and back and back, no further could one go, in infinite regression. The child of king and queen flew up like ancient heroes: his manufactured wings of polished feathers, however close they scythed into the sun, remained in action — unburned, unburied, undevoured by the sharp light. Only his father, uncomprehending, broke down without even departing his laboratory. Fell where he stood before his crucibles, with all his decorations on his chest. A hero of old wars no one wished to remember.

Of the divine retort, she had not left a fragment reconstructed to prove her lineage or her birth. Of the great halls of her man's palaces, she had not left a single column standing. All temples derelict upon their fields of marigolds: the marble pediments like giant bones among the heathers. Had she once reconnoitered that massive city, war magnet to all men from all our islands? Some doubt it to this day. Some say she lived under quite other skies dreaming her daybreak. And then, among the dead, opposing kings had come to gain her hand — and one, the brightest shooting star, had won her gratitude. While we remained at home, love traveled in her, subduing the known world. In her devouring wake, all elements were seen to disappear; all mountains drowned; all humans saved and taken home. Except ourselves.

That day spent drawing angels. Swirling around our mountains here out west, their clouding robes, their limbs like storms inside the robes. No place elsewhere in all the world owns quite such cloudscapes. We had been studying memory's books to ventilate the history of being. We threatened to examine an entire range of mortal happiness, hidden by screens now — screen after screen — but like to break into a nakedness, pregnant and all-revealing. There was some new desire in mind for earth. We ate our hearts out while giving them to eat, so that the multitudes could come to us and live. We had just reached those foothills beyond which going back would not be possible from off the mountains. The mountains breathed contempt for this our life.

Hope wept within our hearts which are her home and tried to take our faces to herself: it was as if she were to come to us, be us entirely. We had not known such hope before. It was as if no hope or joy had been a possibility in all our lives, still could not be and yet — here in the work, and in the work on work, and work on work on work (that marriage eden, fulfilled yet unconsolable) — they stood their ground, their gaze for all of this while on the mountains. Where long before our winter's end, quite contrary to expectation, came all the signs of spring: which first was witnessed in circling clouds ringing the nipples of the mountains. First will be visible and then the flying after.

Which goes before her. O love which never has been penned of any other, the afterghost of hope in my frail image, how she remains until this very day, housed in this mind! We are the afterbirth of time — and here, in our extremity, she takes us up and feeds on us, our hearts and all our organs. We are devoured by this sweet angel of the sun, light of the universe. Not our pale sun ringing our fallen system — but that immense imagination outside the boundaries of any stars, where we may have our bliss in days to come. O widowed eyes that have not seen your peace, your charming soul already knows the home where we must reach to give up all this striving. That sun will slam into this earth, into all earths, take all things back, named and unnamed, to the far edges of eternity. And then, she will remember us and keep her pledge.

ARC 70 : 94

Lift the veil. See the body underneath. See the born beauty of the day revealed that started with such hope. There is so little time before night falls. In my ending is despair said the philosopher: lovers denied him. Despair — but let it not appear so. Appearance is the be-all and the end-all in our work, is it not so? We are the men of confidence, her hopeful suitors, her loving cavaliers. No: see the day and tell of it as if it were the finest of your life, as if many a day were similar to it, as if you knew contentment. And could provoke it. Good morning, Grandfather: to the pinyon tree. Good morning, Grandmother: to the juniper. So would it be throughout day, week, month, year, the learned lifetime. Desire would make it so.

One day the anger will have ended and love will have shone through. All screens will then have fallen. Because you will have known so long our tragedy, our quest so desperate, our almost irretrievable disaster, the love will have shone through, the sad fate shared. Nothing will have been promised in return. It is not possible to set out loving and to expect an answer to that love; there is no guarantee of it, any of it. The love is not returned. You die there long and last without return. Only that anger should have gone — and absolution. That nothing dark remain upon the head of the beloved when no return is made. That the beloved maintain distance and solitary splendor. This as the only task of hope.

She will have broken through at last. Millennium on millennium — and no sign of her. That head in darkness, that miraculous body, those feet, the wave treaders, who walked on water. The miraculous mind, invisible, thinking its planetary thoughts; that mother of all things: created, uncreated, born, coming to be born, not being born for ages, and to be born right at the end of time. Her laughter falling through these clouds, rising from steam over the waters. Step after step, step after step, the movement steady, not up, not down. Yet, a slight up, mostly suggestion, the way we apprehend it, there is no other. The veil is drawn over despair, falls on that death head, closes those vacant eyes. Despair no longer present. Spring in the famished mind, the leaves starting to form, infinitesimal, the flowers coming up over the graves. No longer hope, no longer love. A presence only. A constant presence.

Biographical Note

Nathaniel Tarn, American, was born in France and raised there, in the U.K. and the U.S. He was educated at Cambridge, the Sorbonne, Yale, Chicago and the London Schools of Economics and of Oriental & African Studies. He is a poet, translator, editor, critic and anthropologist. He has published some twenty five books of poetry and translation, has given hundreds of readings in the U.S. and abroad and serves as contributing editor on half a dozen literary magazines. His poetry has been translated into over fifteen foreign languages.

As a translator, he is known for his work on Pablo Neruda, Victor Segalen, the Maya Rabinal Achi and many younger poets. In an interval between academic careers at Chicago, London, Princeton, Pennsylvania, Colorado, Jilin (PRC) and Rutgers Universities, he was Founding General Editor of Cape Editions and Founding Editor of the Cape Goliard Press at Jonathan Cape, London, and Richard Grossman, New York. As a field anthropologist, he has specialized in Highland Maya studies and the sociology of Buddhist institutions, especially in S.E. Asia, with survey work in Alaska, Mexico, China, Japan and the Himalayas. Extended commentaries on his work have appeared over time in *Boundary2; Boxkite* (Sydney); *Jacket* (Internet), *Cross Cultural Poetics* (Minneapolis) and a variety of books.

Tarn's two most recent works are *Scandals in the House of Birds: Shamans and Priests on Lake Atitlan, Guatemala* and a fine letterpress edition of the first seven *Architextures* from the Ninja Press, Sherman Oaks. *Three Letters from the City: the St.Petersburg Poems 1968-98* have been translated into Russian and are forthcoming in a bilingual edition.

For the last five years, Tarn has been immersed in Russian history, culture and current affairs with frequent trips to Russia and ex-Soviet areas. He is a bibliophile and art lover, an amateur aviation historian, an inveterate collector of an intolerable number of minor heraldic objects and an anxious grower of roses. Since 1985, he has lived with his wife Janet Rodney, poet, artist and printer, North of Santa Fe, New Mexico, well clear of the city and attended by an entourage of dogs, coyotes, packrats, field mice, rattlers, tarantulas, black widows and sundry avian creatures.

Other Books From Chax Press

Lisa Cooper, *The Ballad in Memory*
Nathaniel Mackey, *Outlantish*
Eli Goldblatt, *Sessions 1-62*
Ron Silliman, *Demo to Ink*
Beverly Dahlen, *A Reading 8-10*
Gil Ott, *Wheel*
Karen Mac Cormack, *Quirks & Quillets*
Susan Bee & Charles Bernstein, *Fool's Gold*
Sheila Murphy, *Teth*
bp Nichol, *Art Facts: A Book of Contexts*
Charles Bernstein, *Four Poems*
L. Evers & F. S. Molina, *Wo'i Bwikam/Coyote Songs*
Mei-mei Berssenbrugge, *Mizu*
Charles Alexander, *Hopeful Buildings*
Lyn Hejinian & Kit Robinson, *Individuals*
Eli Goldblatt, *Sessions*
John Randolph Hall, *Zootaxy*
Paul Metcalf, *Firebird*
Karl Young, *Five Kwaidan in Sleeve Pages*
Anne Kingsbury, *Journal Entries*
Charles Alexander, *Two Songs*
Paul Metcalf, *Golden Delicious*
Jackson Mac Low, *French Sonnets*